Five Percenter Social Theory
A conceptual-based cultural framework
~Quanaah Publishing~

Quanaah Publishing
www.quanaah-publishing.com

Five Percenter Social Theory
©Copyright 2015
Quanaah Publishing

ALL RIGHTS RESERVED
No portion of this Manual may be reproduced, stored in any electronic system, or transmitted in any form or by any means, electronic, mechanical, photocopy, recording, or otherwise, without written permission from the Author. Brief quotations may be used in literary reviews.

Written/Edited by S. Quanaah
Cover Design by S. Quanaah

-FOR TRAINING AND PUBLIC SPEAKING INFO-

S. Quanaah
EMAIL: atlantisbuild@gmail.com

www.atlantisschool.blogspot.com
www.youtube.com/quanaah
www.soundcloud.com/atlantisbuild

Printed in
The United States of America

Introduction

The purpose of this book is to share a conceptual-based cultural framework of Knowledge of Self [KOS]. This framework is written to examine social phenomena and guide those who are on the path of growth and development. "Five Percenter Social Theory" encompasses ideas about how societies change and develop, psychological/social behavior, power dynamics, social structure and the science of everything in life from the cultural perspective of a Five Percenter.

-S. Quanaah

Saladin Q. Allah
for
Niagara County Legislature

FOR IMMEDIATE RELEASE: July 8th, 2013

Youth Mentor, Published Author, and Community Activist Saladin Q. Allah has announced his candidacy for the Fourth District Niagara County Legislature seat in the city of Niagara Falls, New York

Niagara Falls, New York -- Saladin Q. Allah said that he is seeking the seat of Fourth District County Legislator because he believes that his vision to expand youth outreach, increase community alliances and initiatives, promote neighborhood safety and crime prevention, and to develop a local living economy is what his district both wants and needs.

"I was born in the City of Niagara Falls into a family of seven," he said. "My parents, Lois and Philip Frank, were pillars within the same Community that I was raised in, and that I am seeking to represent as our next Niagara County Legislator."

Allah said that he knows what it is to both struggle and serve; and he believes that his parents set a great example for him in that his mother, Lois Frank, received her Bachelor's of Arts Degree from Niagara University at the age of forty-two, majoring in psychology and a minoring in sociology. She had seven children at that time and she went on to become a case manager for both Community Missions and for Family and Children's Services. She later served as a Director of the Niagara Community Center.

Allah's father, Philip Frank, served as a member of the National Guard and completed a machinist apprenticeship program during his twelve-years working at Carborundum. Philip later became a member of the Painters Union Local for another twelve years.

Just as Allah is proud of the example that his parents set, he is just as proud as the one Josiah Henson, his great-great-great grandfather, set was a forerunner of the Underground Railroad. Harriet Beecher Stowe merged elements of Henson's life into her popular anti-slavery novel Uncle Tom's Cabin, which inspired the abolitionist of President Lincoln's day to rail against slavery, setting into motion the end of that kind of America. Henson later established a community for fugitive slaves called the Dawn Settlement, and he founded the British-American Institute in Dresden, ON.

Allah said that it is through those members of his family that he learned the value of education, a strong work ethic, sacrifice, and teamwork. He believes those to be the same vital building blocks of any successful community.

"I attended Central State University in Wilberforce OH," Allah said, "as a therapeutic recreation major, and since returning to WNY, I've been invested in our community from the grassroots level, working particularly with our youth.

Allah said that he has been doing youth outreach by creating successful mentorship programs and assisting with other community youth projects for over fifteen years.

"I've shown my commitment to our youth and my confidences are in their ability to one day lead our communities when given the continual support and guidance they need." That's why he said that he is a strong advocated for the reopening of the Niagara Community Center in the city's north end and instituting anti-bullying campaigns.

Allah, a published author, added, "Professionally, I've self-published ten books that explores various social issues, and have worked as a program consultant for an episode on the History Channel's show, Gangland.

But it was not enough that he is published, he sponsors young writers programs to help others to do so, too. Some people, he said, may know him from his National Prison Correspondence and Book Donation Program, or have heard him as a guest speaker at several national colleges.

As his forbearers have instilled values in him, he has likewise instilled similar values in his two daughters. One is a recent high school graduate who has earned a lacrosse scholarship to Howard University; and the other is an eleventh grade honor student, whose goal is to become a local business owner.

Allah believes that as the next Fourth District County Legislator that he will have a larger platform to better serve our community. "We need leadership that understands that a seat and a voice is still not enough at the table. We need leadership with an activist spirit, someone with an actual agenda and work ethic to help transform our collective quality of life. Together, the community and I, are that kind of leadership."

Allah further said that crime prevention starts with us. He said that, "The crimes in our neighborhoods are primarily committed by relatives or people we know, not people who are unknown. We need members who are willing to protect our most vulnerable members: children, women, seniors, and the handicapped."

Allah concluded, "As our next county legislator I will remain transparent, accessible, and responsive to our district, because I am for the people. You will still see me utilizing our resources at our local public library, playing basketball with our youth at Legends Park, and proactively involved in community functions. I will also hold local community circles; forums designed to keep people informed about community and legislative issues, and I will seek input on issues related to our city and county. For the future of our youth, community, and the city of Niagara Falls, I look forward to speaking with you in the coming months, and I will fully earn your vote of conscience, and confidence.

The Babies Are The Greatest!

If I'm a parent, teaching my own children is expected, not something I should be looking to get credit for as an accomplishment. In my experience, I've ceen the phrase, "I'm teaching my children" expressed by people for a few basic reasons:

1.) They're new parents experiencing a parental role for the first time, so they're proudly sharing what they do.

2.) They're people who've had some parenting issues in the past, for whatever reason, so they're seeking validation.

3.) They're people trying to use what they're doing for their children as an excuse (shield) to not do anything for others.

Regardless of these or other reasons, saying "I teach my children" is no different than saying, "I feed my children." As their parent, we're supposed to do that, b.u.t. it does take our collective parental efforts to teach, and feed, our children consistently. This requires love and consideration beyond our personal household.

Gaining Knowledge of Self naturally expands our perspective of civilization and our duty as pivilized people. As this expansion of consciousness happens with us as parents, we begin to look beyond the creature comforts of our own front door, our personal household, and the limitations of a "me and mines" philosophy; a philosophy that cannot address the greater needs we're now aware of amongst our children's peers and within our neighborhood/community. So we start moving away from exclusively saying "My child(ren)" to now inclusively saying "our children." We begin to recognize that "the babies" are the greatest, not just our own child(ren). We transition from simply being a father or mother to our own children to being a father to the fatherless and mother to the motherless.

This expansion of consciousness is an important part of our growth and development process and evolution as parents; it represents the "It takes a village" mentality/approach we need to continually inspire, empower, and educate our children to build a more sustainable future. All of us have benefitted from this mentality/approach in some way, and our children are the beneficiaries, in need of this today.

Community Circles

-How The Mighty Have Fallen-

Our communities are not destroyed for lack of knowledge. People know what's wrong, especially those of us who live within the community, that confront these problems each and every day. Our communities are apathetically destroyed for lack of sacrifice. Many of us are simply unwilling to look out for one another, even our own children, in order to secure personal possessions and creature comforts for ourselves.

My father, Philip Frank, is a painter by trade and an artist/musician at heart. As a teenager he played the bass in a group called The El Moroccos. It was my father's influence where I developed a great love for music, nature, and culture. In second grade when I was asked what I wanted to be when I grew up I told my teacher Mrs. Smith, "a Zoologist!" My favorite animal was a 'jaguarundi' and my father, my twin brothers, and myself would watch animal/nature programs religiously. Whether it was National Geographic, Wild America, Nova, Wild Wild World of Animals and etc., if it was on, we saw it. My father also collected African art and taught us about our classical civilizations and cultural traditions prior to slavery. Recognizing the Dinka tribe from the Masai tribe, learning the story of General Hannibal, and understanding our story in America was common knowledge in our household. I also learned that I am the great-great-great grandson of Josiah Henson; forerunner of the Underground Railroad, founder of a Community of fugitive slaves in Dresden, Ontario Canada and the British-American Vocational Institute. It was through my father that I gained my cultural consciousness and developed my interpersonal relationship with the planet.

My mother, Lois Frank, was a psychologist/sociologist by trade. One of my earliest memories of her is being gathering up on rainy days with a few of my siblings and put into our Pontiac Grand Safari to go look for "our buddies". She'd drive us around the city until we found our buddies and once we saw them she would tell us to wave, and we would return home. Our buddies were a group of four homeless people who sought shelter from the rain underneath an overpass. Over time, my siblings and I began to initiate these outings by asking our mother could we go look for our buddies when it rained. With that simple gesture, our mother successfully taught us to identify with others and a social condition synonymous with rain. Years later I would implement the same parenting techniques by taking my school age daughters to "the lunch place". Nine years later my eldest daughter, Asiyah, would write about these experiences, the people she met, and how this positively shaped her life on college entry essays. All this time she never knew that the lunch place was the community soup kitchen. Asiyah is now graduating High School and will be pursuing a career in forensic psychology at Howard University in our nation's capitol. It was through my mother that I gained my social consciousness and developed my interpersonal relationship to the world.

Along my journey there are many who have added onto and reinforced the foundation my parents have laid. Those people who have played and often still play the most significant roles in my growth and development have been people who understood the meaning of sacrifice. From my eldest sibling Brad Frank who would invest his own money and get resources to train my peers and I in the summer for the upcoming football season, to Rev. Kenneth James who kept his office, church, and home open to us who were seeking guidance and support in becoming boys to men. There were business owners like Carmen Jones, Mr. Brown, Beechie, Mr. Williamson, Arthur Ray, Howard, Ms. Theresa, Ms. Price and etc., youth advocates like Knuckles, Virgil, Greg Lewis, Reggie McCreary, Hamp, Garth and various others too numerous to mention who took ownership of our neighborhoods and sacrificed their personal time and finances to insure that my present generation would be here today. It was through their collective work, responsibility and examples that I understand what community is about, and I actively build upon this legacy with the things that I do.

One thing that I've found in common with all of the people that I mentioned above was their sense of sacrifice. As business owners it was never about making themselves rich off of the support from the community. It was about providing a service and reciprocating the money the community paid for these services by supporting other businesses, organizations and institutions within our community; Beechie would buy groceries at Mr. Brown's store down the block and Mr. Brown would get his hair cut at Beechie's Barbershop. Our dollar circulated a few times before leaving our community and this type of support for one another strengthened the socioeconomic integrity of our families and thus our community as a whole. We sacrificed personal gains to ensure that we collectively prospered.

I was recently asked, "What type of vision do I have for our community?" My answer is that is, I have the same vision as those who came before me. The same vision I benefited from that I share with my own children and our present generation: our greatest natural resource and ambassadors of the future. I see people taking more pride in our community because they're home owners. I see people who were once discriminated against because of a non-violent offense they committed fifteen years ago being business owners, employed, and providing a service to a neighborhood they once took from. I see Sunday no longer being the most segregated day of the week because our religious community is now working as a community; collectively supporting, protecting, and providing programs and activities for the most vulnerable elements of our society: women, children, seniors, the poor/unemployed, and the handicapped. I see our community no longer relying on an underfunded, understaffed police force to resolve all our problems and keep our neighborhoods safe from ourselves. I see us policing ourselves, as guardian angels, who have taken an active stance against crime, juvenile delinquency, and family dysfunction. I see our community investing in our youth by supporting the cultural arts, recreation centers, entertainment, and educational opportunities that encourage their positive growth & development. Lastly and most importantly, I see our community as ours; a place our ancestors migrated to with goals of building, supporting, and perpetuating a better life for each other.

The decline of any community is marked by its member's unwillingness and inability to protect and provide for its most vulnerable elements: women, children, seniors, the poor/unemployed, and the handicapped. Establishing resources to protect and provide for these family elements builds the compound called a community. In order to restore this place, we must be willing and able to sacrifice the "I" for "we", the "mine" for "ours", and the "me & you" for "us". If we all do a little, no one needs to do a lot. In the rebuilding process one of our greatest enemies is apathy; the lack of interest, enthusiasm, or concern for each other and rebuilding our community. Many of our politicians, clergy, parents, businesses and organizations are apathetic. It's impossible for a community to deteriorate, on the watch of those who care. When we care we're concerned. Concern means we're able to relate and when we're able to relate we can establish relationships; the intimate glue that holds our families, neighborhoods, and communities together. This is a rebuilding process that doesn't happen over night. It's a long term investment in each other, and more specifically our children. It's the type of posture that inspires, empowers, and educates our children to develop a relationship with our community. It's also the type of posture that encourages our children to take ownership of our community when we are no longer here. I am the result of this posture and learned, through the sacrifice of others, my role, relationship and responsibility to our community. After studying therapeutic recreation at Central State University in Wilberforce, OH, I returned to WNY and have diligently worked as a youth advocate for over a decade. I have authored/published several books on the subject of social commentary, worked as a program consultant for an episode of the History Channel Series 'Gangland', started a Prison Correspondence Project, created/financed various other initiatives/programs and have partnered with many Institutions that advocate for the same common community causes. While many have praised me for these efforts I constantly remind them that I am because we are. I am the result of many others, known and unknown, who have sacrificed their time, finances, and lives to pave the way for me to have these opportunities to contribute to a rich ancestral legacy. I am not apathetic because I saw many who cared and demonstrated their love for one another.

When a community doesn't function as a circle-like ecosystem of positive human resources, it simply becomes a negative, vicious, parasitic cycle amongst its members. If we, as members of our community, are apathetic about the process of building it, we are the very elements that bring about its destruction. In conclusion, I leave you all with this question: What type of vision do you have for our community, and what sacrifices are you willing/able to make to help bring this vision to life?

Marquise de Merteuil and Cécile de Volanges

Misogyny = Misandry

Western society, without a doubt, is historically and presently misogynistic, male chauvinistic, sexist and gender oppressive. I've never supported this and have always been a firm advocate of equality, regardless of gender. Many others also bear witness to this inherent problem with western society yet the important question to ask ourselves is, "What are we doing about it?" For females, this question is even more critical to answer because through her is potentially born the solution to these social ills.

There are females who have taken and are taking successful steps to solve this problem via embracing cultures that are non-western, engaging in the political process to create legislation that brings about levels of equality, and creating their own institutions/businesses that promotes gender equality. At the same time you have other females who haven't taken successful steps to solve this problem. So instead of addressing misogyny they become misandrists; an unhealthy response to an unhealthy situation.

Misandry is defined as "*hatred or strong dislike for males, boys, and men*". The word "misandry" didn't appear in most dictionaries until the mid 1900's and in the 1970's it was considered a new term being introduced into mainstream American English (language). Misandry, as a concept, still hasn't been totally aknowledged within mainstream western society because if you were to go to Microsoft Word right now and type in the word "misandrist" a red line will appear underneath it meaning 'this is not a word' or 'this word is mispelled'. The point here to consider is that words, and their function, still shape our reality -even if Microsoft Word doesn't acknowledge them. It's also important to consider that just because words are not common within mainstream American English, it doesn't mean they don't exist, they're harmless, or neutral. In fact, oftentimes it's those things that appear nonexistent, innocent, and indifferent that actually end up being the most real, harmful, and political.

There are many reasons, in addition to a misogynistic western societal atmosphere, that females become misandrists. Sometimes they were raised by lesbian parents. Other times they may have been taken advantage of or abandoned by the males in their life. Maybe they were influenced by a feminist. Perhaps they were in relationships with serial cheaters. Regardless what their rationalization is for this contempt for males, it doesn't solve their problem of reconciliation. Over the years I've watched females group together based upon mutual pain and insecurities. Many of these support groups are often nothing more than bitch sessions to trade war stories about mental, emotional, and physical abuse. Many of these groups do not even consider or explore healthy ways to reconcile a dysfunctional family unit and bring males and females back together. Oftentimes their mission statements are "It's all about my sisters" and the background music is the Covergirl, Queen Latifiahed theme from Living Single. There's nothing wrong with sisterhood; I think that's very important for our families and communities! Yet when these girlfriend pow-pows are not providing females with effective/healthy ways to come together with males to advocate one common cause of (re)building a family and community, that's a fundamental problem.

Whenever I engage a group of females who're advocating any kind of woman's group I always ask them what is their plan of action and goal in regards to coming together with males/men for the purpose of family and community. If they don't have a plan, goal or even try to rationalize their mission as "*focused on what females/women need to do for ourselves*" I know right then and there that I, as a male/man, am not an essential part of their plan or goal in regards to family and community. This mentality and approach is no different than the plans of action western society has historically advocated with no goal for coming together with black/brown families and communities. In other words, Caucasians as a group in America, have historically and legally kept black/brown apart from their own social equality from 1776-1965; 189 years of America's 237 year existence. Instead of finding healthy ways to address this alienation/seperation, many black/brown people have adopted the same mentality and approach towards eachother. So many of us keep eachother apart from our own social equality based upon cultural, ethnic, religious, academic, economic, gender, and etc. differences too. One of these differences I am pointing out is along gender lines; where black/brown females, in response to the 'blackfaced misogyny' that may or may not have been directly and indirectly perpetrated against them by black/brown males, are now promoting Misandry.

Many females don't even realize that deep down inside they're holding this contempt for males, boys, and men. One of the biggest indicators is when the bulk of their conversation is about how worthless males are and how men are beneath them. It reminds me of this female having a conversation with me about how dudes just wasn't on her level, as if she was The Last Unicorn. I perfectly understand the frustration of socializing with 'some' people; I've gotten frustrated myself. Yet to take a position that "males", "men", and "dudes" are ALL a certain way is deeply problematic. The females who think and feel this way about ALL males have basically reduced themselves to three abiological options in life:

1.) Denounce all males and become a lesbian.
2.) Denounce all males, become a female eunuch, and promote fratricide/patricide.
3.) Use males as a tool and also as a slave.

While the issue of gender equality is a legitimate concern for any female (and males), these three abiological choices are not a healthy response/answer to the problem of misogyny. They're not legitimate solutions because they do not demonstrate a female's commitment to assist in (re)building families and communities for our future generations. For without males there are no children or future and a society without offspring will cease to exist; just like societies without females to bear offspring will also cease to exist. So ceeing that these three options are obviously not a healthy response/answer, what is a legitimate solution to the problem? Do these solutions insure the production, provisions, and protection of a future society?

I think before we even answer that question we have to be aware that we, as black/brown people within North America, are not the primary architects of this society. We were given legal permission to participate in this society about 48 years ago -even though America will be celebrating its 239th birthday this year. So we as black/brown people are not the status quo nor does this society we reside in primarily reflect our ancestor's culture (core values, language, customs, traditions and etc.). Because we reside in North America and were subjected to its cultural conditions, all of us in some form or fashion have adopted many of these core values, language, customs, traditions and etc. We we all assimilated and some of us are striving daily to recapture our culture. So this is the lens we should be looking at eachother through; a filter of consideration for being made other than ourselves from eating the wrong cultural foods. In other words, present day black/brown males who perpetuate western society's misogyny, male chauvinism, sexism and gender oppression were taught this from the most misogynistic, male chauvinist, sexist and gender oppressive people on the planet. Likewise, black/brown females whose unhealthy answer to misandry (and misogyny) are also perpetuating a western ideology. Realizing this gives us the ability think about and seek answers outside of the western box many of us are stuck in. In thinking outside of the box we must ask ourselves: How did we relate to eachother as black/brown people before July 4th 1776? How did we relate to one another 1200 years ago? What about 10,000 years ago? The further we go back, the resources/references we have to solve the problems of today. In many cases we'll come across practical solutions from people who thought about our problems many moons ago.

In closing, I want to encourage my sisters (and brothers) to realize that whatever problems we face as a people today doesn't exist in a vacuum. Also, the problems we're thinking about today are problems we have already considered; archeologists have documented us as being here hundreds of thousands of years so that's alot of thinking about life and living. In striving to solve our problems, any solutions we come up with MUST involve a commitment to assist in (re)building our families and communities for our future generations. If this bond is not present, our lives will continue to be broken. Again, we've been documented as being here for hundreds of thousands of years so there are plenty of examples to put our theories to the test. Misogyny and misandry is flawed logic; there is no life that has ever come from that. Hatred, strong dislike, or disatisfaction with one another only breeds dissention. This dissention causes division and before long we make devils. Ladies, yes there are males who need some work, just like you do, and we need to work it out together. It's an excellent idea to come together as women/sisters to address issues related to a female b.u.t. don't forget about us males. We need your insight and answers about ways we can (re)build our families and communities; our future generations depend on us providing these answers, together.

Hip Hop Culture 101

-In Defense of Lord Jamar-

I recently read an article by Michael Muhammad Knight entitled "Kanye West in a kilt has Lord Jamar so hard right now" that was in response to Lord Jamar's recent Tweets, Vlad TV Interview and New Song entitled "Lift Up Your Skirt." Lift Up Your Skirt was inspired by Lord Jamar's stance on the skirt/kilt Kanye West -in particular- has recently worn, skinny jeans and ultimately the effeminization of males in HipHop Culture. After reading Knight's article I was compelled to further add-on about what I understand this issue to be.

One of the things that many people need to first consider about Hip Hop is that it's a culture, meaning "a way of life". This way of living is comprised of various elements such as breakin (dance), emceeing, graffiti art, deejaying, beatboxing, fashion, language, knowledge, entrepreneurialism and any other components that make it a culture. These elements were first forged and defined as a culture by black/brown youth within the inner cities of New York, beginning in the Bronx. This definition did not come from thin air or a position of privilege or entitlement; it arose out of a position/condition of making a way out of no way. The founders of Hip Hop culture were black/brown youth; the children of the segregation/civil rights/black power movement and oppressed/colonized people from the islands. As the children of these conditions, our goal was never cultural assimilation or seeking acceptance/validation from a western society that rejected us; we created our own way of life. So this way of life or culture we call Hip Hop was born out of the socioeconomic, cultural and geopolitical considerations (and influences) of our fore parents, our chronology and our environment. This is one reason "sampling" has always been a part of Hip Hop culture; it demonstrates that connection to the chronology, cultural roots and musical contributions of our fore parents. This does not mean that there were NO Caucasians present because some did participate. This only means that we, black/brown people, were and still are the first world (indigenous) people of Hip Hop culture; not the minority, second class citizens or third world people. The only reason Hip Hop is present today is because it was passed on from one generation to the next. It was this form of cultural propagation that made this reproduction possible. So from a cultural perspective, there have always been principles and core values to ensure the birth of Hip Hop's future "offspring." There have also been foreign values outside of Hip Hop that were never advocated because they would not ensure the birth of Hip Hop's future "offspring". So Hip Hop today, in 2013, is now a global phenomenon and this is because of its cultural virility (power to procreate) and fertility (power to produce).

Lord Jamar Allah

Lord Jamar spoke clearly on how the effeminization of males within Hip Hop in particular (via skinny jeans, skirts/kilts and etc.) is the result of foreign values being injected into this culture that is altering its course and potential to reproduce. In other words, he was pointing out the cross-pollination of values going on between Hip Hop culture and western society. He argued that this effeminization is a process and practice that is causing a Hip Hop cultural genocide. He also pointed out that effeminization has never been a part of core values of Hip Hop culture, nor has it ever been reflected in the social norms/more of those who live this way of life. However, we do cee this process and practice as an acceptable "lifestyle" norm within western society at large. For example: homosexuality, as a practice, is no longer defined as a mental disorder (per the DSM-IV) but a lifestyle that western society openly embraces; although this style, defined as life, does not actually propagate life. In other words, if all of us chose to practice homosexuality right now, there would not be another generation of human beings on the planet once we die. All opinions and feelings about homosexuality aside, that is the genealogical reality; this practice violates the first law of nature: self preservation. The only option for those who do choose to practice homosexuality is to manufacture artificial means to propagate life such as: the building of sperm banks, in vitro fertilization, surrogacy, human cloning and etc. As western society continues to inject its values within Hip Hop, also consider what artificial means (people, places and things) it likewise employs to propagate its life.

Some people feel and/or think Lord Jamar's stance was a personal attack against homosexuals. No, his stance was for the conservation, production and perpetuation of a culture he and other black/brown people created -that has now gotten into the hands of cultural bandits. Kanye West and various other entertainers are the ambassadors of these bandits and use their status within western society to primarily reinforce its values, not the cultural principles and core values of Hip Hop's first world (indigenous) people. I know the difference because I am the younger sibling of the youth who created Hip Hop culture. Yet what about the youth of today? Would they know the difference between Hip Hop's core values and western society's foreign values being injected in our culture? Those who know our chronology probably do. Those who don't know this chronology typically look at Kanye West, A$AP Rocky, P-Diddy and other entertainers choices as a simple fashion statement, not a declaration of independence from an indigenous Hip Hop nation. Lord Jamar was not the first person to raise the issue against cultural assimilation; this stance was present in HipHop's inception and was always reflected in its various "counter-culture" elements -as western society deemed them. It was only when western corporate interests saw that they could make money from Hip Hop that they eventually began separating emceeing and deejaying from the other elements in order to get paid. And if the rap didn't coincide with those interests they either didn't promote it, undermined it or simply paid "sellouts" (as we called them) to do it. This is still the corporate formula of today and even though the term sellout has become archaic amongst the present generation, Sellouts still functionally exist.

In closing, keep in mind that Hip Hop as a culture is now becoming a global phenomenon that is primarily in the hands of western corporate interests. These interests primarily reflect the core values of the west yet many of Hip Hop's indigenous people (and progeny) have bought into these values and dance to the tune these corporate pipers are playing. The euro-centered materialism, objectification of women, effeminization of males, rugged individualism and etc. are all examples of acultural elements that never represented the roots of Hip Hop culture. Within this culture we always had proverbial wisdom, colloquialisms and slang that reinforced our core values. "Biting" meant to be original and not copy. "crossover" meant to keep our culture originally Hip Hop, not assimilate or become 'Pop' (popular culture). These, and various other terms/phrases, reflect core values a lot of the present generation is no longer aware of and do not advocate. These, and various other terms/phrases, are not reflected in alot of the mainstream rap music or advocated by many entertainers that are supported by western corporate interests. An example of this is how this society originally declared the Hip Hop elements emceeing and deejaying as "Jungle Music" and refused to play it on the radio. Michael Muhammad Knight's article clearly reflected a lack of awareness/connection with the chronology of Hip Hop culture and the social norms/mores that helped transmit this way of life from one generation to the next.

While many of these social norms/mores were overt, much of the culture was covert and transmitted non-verbally; unspoken rules and regulations the indigenous people of Hip Hop forged and understood amongst ourselves. Those on the outside looking in aren't privy to this culture's social norms/mores, especially the unspoken rules and regulations. Therefore, they tend to categorize Hip Hop not as a culture but as an 'art' that simply promotes 'freedom of expression'; a common phrase and buzzword associated with the LGBT community. To the contrary, Hip Hop has only supported freedom within the context of our cultural worldview; a view that was rarely advocated or reflected in the western society around us. Anything we considered culturally 'out of bounds' was considered "wack", meaning corny or not legit, and those who were saying/doing wack stuff were strait "buggin!" Again, many of these, and various other terms/phrases, are not reflected in a lot of the mainstream rap music today. So obviously many of the concepts and core values that reinforce this language aren't present. Lord Jamar's stance and many others within our Hip Hop community is much more insightful than "policing fabric" as Knight stated, nor does it have anything to do with Prophet Muhammad sitting down to use the bathroom or being, as western society has coined, "homophobic." In plain ole Hip Hop language, Lord Jamar was just reiterating the same sentiments Hip Hop culture has always held since its inception: Kanye West and various other entertainers are biting western society and that crossover stuff is wack! They may be talented artists but they're bugging because their choices are clearly leading our present generation and our future generations down a path of Hip Hop cultural genocide.

On Outsiders

As a public figure I've learned alot and continue to learn alot when it comes to effective public speaking and basic public relationship skills. One of the things I've definately learned about this platform is how to choose battles. A few years back I had an incident where I gave people alittle too much credit by even mentioning their name and putting to rest their accusations against me. It's a situation I could have ignored like it was pork yet I chose to take it on. A couple years after that another incident occurred and I took the "ignore it like it is pork" approach instead. It was pretty difficult going through it without giving any time, attention or energy into it. Although I took two different approaches, the results of both incidents are exactly the same; I continue to add-on and remain a relevant contributor to the growth and development of people throughtout the World. With the worldwide web there's many opportunities for people to put on facades, front, create illusions and manipulate others into buying into their BS. So one of the reasons I've consistently operated this A.S.I.A. Journal is to remain a beacon of light for those who're seeking real growth and development, not facades, fronting, illusions and manipulation.

The last article I wrote, Hip Hop Culture 101: in Defense of Lord Jamar elaborated on various attacks on Lord Jamar's position in regards to his reasoning for his song "Lift Up Your Skirt". Lord Jamar, one of the group members of Brand Nubian; contributing architects of Golden Era conscious Hip Hop, were very inspirational in my growth and development. So I was motivated to clarify some of the stances he took and to also address some of the criticisms he received from "outsiders" of that culture. One of these outsiders and main criticizers is also an outsider of the primary culture/society that Lord Jamar, myself and others subscribe to and are active citizens of.

One of the things you'll notice in all of this, whether we're dealing with Hip Hop or the Nation of Gods and Earths (The NGE/Five Percenters), is outside opinions. Some years back I posted a video on A.S.I.A. entitled "Nuuwabians, Hebrews, Muslims, Khemetians, etc..?" The purpose of that was to emphasize that if anyone wants to know what these groups teach then go directly to them to learn. It seems simple enough b.u.t. time and time again people choose to get their information from "outsiders" instead of going directly to the source. This isn't to say that an outsider doesn't know anything, they may, in theory. Yet if you want to know about some of the ins and outs of prison doesn't it make sense to learn directly from someone who's been a career criminal and incarcerated in 5 or 6 different medium/maximum facilities? Or would you rather your primary source be someone who's only gotten a jaywalking ticket in their life and has a DVD collection of Gangland? Again, this is not to say you can't learn ANYTHING from the later person; most times you'll learn that this person can tell you some things about the map yet is completely oblivious to the terrain because they never actually been there...

Because we, as black/brown people, are the minority group here in the wilderness of North America, everything we do is going to be critiqued from the outside society we live in. That's a given. The various different cultural societies that further makes a minority further compounds this critique. That's also a given. So in considering this, we can either obsess over what outsiders think or we can continue to do what we've been doing knowing that outsiders are going to think what they want anyway. It's all about choosing our battles; sometimes issues need to be addressed directly and other times we need to ignore it like it is pork. This incident has been a wake up call for many of us who have sat by and not taken the necessary measures to preserve and protect our culture, whether that's Hip Hop or the Nation of Gods and Earths. So today I want to share a couple key points in regards to that preservation and protection.

There was never a time in our nation's chronology where our general consensus towards teaching others was, "Who wants to be a Five Percenter raise their hand?" People had to earn the right to be trusted with our brother/sisterhood and these teachings we hold as sacred. Nowadays people are handing out lessons like they're pitchin' mollies from the corner and we wonder why people can claim to be the God or Earth so and so yet doing THIS the other days of the week. In the early days of our nation (circa the 1960's to the 1980's), we didn't allow outsiders to just come amongst us nor did we give outsiders the symbolic authority to move the furniture around in our house.

We didn't allow people to audio/video record our rallies, parliaments or events. We didn't publish books and only wrote our understanding concerning our lessons/mathematics in plus degrees that we internally circulate(d) amongst ourselves. These protocols kept many people from infiltrating us. Although the growth of the internet and social networking may give outsiders the impression that The NGE and learning our culture is easily accessible and one or two videos, downloads, amazon purchases and google searches away from being a Five Percenter, that is absolutely untrue. With the exception of audio/video recording some of our rallies, parliaments or events and publishing some books, many of us still adhere to many of these standards we practiced in the early days concerning outsiders and the outside world.

In The NGE there are certain customs, traditions, principles, values, protocols, rules and regulations we strive to collectively adhere to. 75%, 6/8th's or the majority of these customs, traditions, principles, values, protocols, rules and regulations are directly derived from our knowledge, wisdom and understanding of 120 lessons, regardless if we're male or female; a Five Percenter is non-gender specific. These protocols are in place as a system of checks and balances to maintain the order of our society. An example of this is a conversation I had with a female who defined herself as "the Earth" for years yet when asked 'What is the duty of a civilized person?' (18/1-40) she didn't even know -just like the average scantly clad, pork eating, 85% female doesn't know that this female often took pride in criticizing: the irony of knowledge build or destroy... It's a problem when the only real difference between people on the so-called inside and outsiders is what they chose to wear and take instagram pictures of that day. If appearance is the face value standard and lackadaisical posture we're using to determine who's who in the zoo, then we will continue to compromise our ability to preserve and protect our culture. Yet if we continue to adhere to the customs, traditions, principles, values, protocols, rules and regulations of our nation such as asking people "How do you cee today's mathematics?", "How do you cee today's degree?", "Do you knowledge 120?", "What degrees are you dealing with?", "How long have you had Knowledge of Self?", "Who is your enlightener/educator?", "Where did you get Knowledge of Self?" and etc.. Everything will come out in the wash. And even if someone answered "The 8th degree in the 1-40's" when asked, "What degrees are you dealing with?" TAKE TIME TO QUIZ THEM SO THEY CAN SHOW AND PROVE IT! They may be honest and sincere. You may also find out that they didn't anticipate you quizzing them and once you start questioning them you'll cee they were either telling a boldface lie or exaggerating what they knew, could accurately recite and actually understood about our culture.

This examination process isn't personal and never was personal; it's nation business. And this examination process extends equally to both males and females; the corresponding, foundational units of our nation, Gods (males) and Earths (females). This is the approach we've always taken to ensure that those who are around us are actually us! This is the approach we've always taken to ensure that our families (especially our children) are protected from outsiders who don't advocate our common cause. This is the approach we've always taken to ensure that you or I can't just say or do anything and think it's acceptable to our group's culture! Unfortunately many people aren't honorable and will try to fake it until they make it so the customs, traditions, principles, values, protocols, rules and regulations of our nation serve IMPARTIAL STANDARDS to ensure our culture is preserved and protected from anyone mixing, diluting and tamering with 'What We Teach' and 'What We Will Achieve.' USE THESE IMPARTIAL STANDARDS by requiring that people know, can articulate and understand these standards or you'll loose it (cultural integrity) -and possibly your life behind claiming outsiders as the same as you. Require that others also hold you to these IMPARTIAL STANDARDS!

People, outsiders, are going to say what they're going to say about us on "the outside". They often do this to lure us into their arena so they can have their way with us on their terms and in their arena; sort of like inviting you on their Show so they can make a Show out of you... Reminds me of the scene in The Wire when Avon Barksdale was schoolin' Stringer about "playing them away games" when he got beat by Senator Clay Davis. When these outsiders come on the inside and feel as though they have some sense of entitlement and authority to say what they want about us it's because we deputized them. Bottom line is we need to tighten up our ranks and stop being so lax about our examination process, internally and with obvious outsiders.

Bridge Mix and Fakebook

I cannot stress enough the importance of properly examining people before allowing them into your social equality and allowing them to simply "claim" they're about the same thing as you. It's likewise important for us to allow ourselves to be examined before coming amongst others. I reside in the WNY/Southern Ontario Area where there isn't a high concentration of Five Percenters like in NYC. This has been a gift yet I've also ceen the curse. The gift is the fact that since some of these areas are unchartered regions, this environment encourages cultural development, self reliance and the propagation of our way of life. On the flip side, those people who really "ain't bout this life" find themselves slipping right back into a dead world or trying to be a cyclops in the land of the blind.

There are people, some who claim to have been around for years, that come in the names of Five Percenters yet when you ask them what lessons they actually know either they hopelessly stumble through reciting them like Leslie Nielson trying to sing the national anthem in The Naked Gun or they reluctantly tell you they've been [stuck] on the same lesson for a while now... It disapppointed me the most when I've heard this coming from those people who portray themselves as Five Percenters and who always have the harshest criticisms about what somebody else ain't doing. The problem is not the fact that they don't know their lessons or the lack of knowledge itself. We all started out from a place of not knowing and there are many things I'm unaware of about life right now b.u.t. the bottom line is, "What are we (am I) doing about it?" The problem arises when people choose to not do anything about it, especially when it's brought to their attention. The problem is their sense of apathy (or apathetic arrogance) and contentment with ignorance. Apathetic arrogance is when apathetic people, who obviously haven't invested the time to study/learn, arrogantly expect all the accreditation and accoutrements of someone who actually invested/invests the time to study/learn (know, articulate and understand the lessons). My point in mentioning this is not for the sake of encouraging these people to get it together; it usually doesn't work that way. Encouragement usually works for people who honestly aren't aware of what they need to be doing and will strive to do better in their own good time when shown the way. The people I'm referring to already know what's up, stubbornly don't want to hear what anyone has to say and may go into a Rowdy Roddy Piper frenzy if you question them. The reason they're in this state is because over a period of time they simply made up a variety of excuses to stagnate -which YOU WILL HEAR when you have a conversation with them about their studies-, instead of healthy adjustments to elevate. Because of their pride, defensiveness and often arrogance they usually won't welcome your line of questioning and try to act like it's a personal attack against them instead of what's really taking place: a confirmation of the Knowledge they clearly aren't adding on to their cipher. So I mention this not for these people. On their own, they have to make the choice to care enough about true growth & development, be concerned enough about the inadequate position it puts them in to assist others (especially their own families) and recognize that knowledge is more valuable and a priority over the Ignorance they own. Our job is to simply make knowledge born, their job is to save themselves.

I'm sharing this with those of you who may have encountered and will encounter these people who are coming in the Name. It's important to realize that regardless of how they dress, the lingo they can talk or names they can drop of people who aren't examining them, they are not you. You can be friendly or associate yet this relationship becomes a liability if you give them more credit than they deserve and expect them to uphold the same cultural principles/values you adhere to. That is an unreasonable expectation you're unfairly placing on them and that relationship. How? Because these people never invested the time and aren't investing the time to learn or adhere to these principles/values you hold sacred. If you're in doubt about what I'm saying simply ask them to go through their lessons and share their understanding and they'll show & prove it to you out of their own mouth. If they don't even know these lessons, how can they possibly understand what they're unaware of or live that out as a consistent code of conduct? This is not to say that ALL PEOPLE who are coming in our names b.u.t. have not fully committed themselves to learning/living our culture are outright despicable, some may be. They may have some nice qualities about themselves and even demonstrate "some" (key word) of the principles/values we advocate as a nation. In my experience with those people who are less likely to take responsibility for themselves and study their lessons, one of their main arguments -in defense of their own ignorance of course-, is "So and so knows 120 frontwards and backwards yet they're doing A, B, C, D, and etc.!" Yes this may be a legitimate point because reciting lessons doesn't automatically mean someone is learning these lessons. Yet talking about somebody else does absolutely nothing to address or resolve the situation at hand: this person's choice to be ignorant and what they're actually doing about it. Even if a Five Percenter who knows 120 is demonstrating questionable behavior, at least I and thousands of other Five Percenters have an impartial, consistent, equitable standard between us (120 lessons) to potentially check and balance our words/behavior. With someone who primarily dresses the part, uses our lingo and name drops you have no impartial, consistent, equitable standard or transparency between you. What you do have, culturally speaking, is big box of Bridge Mix; a variety of nuts, fruit and cremes 'covered' with milk and dark chocolate -and you never know what you're going to get or where it comes from! Bottom line is it's important to hold fast to our customary tradition of "examining and being examined". Without this protocol we will continue to cee our cultural Integrity being compromised.

Speaking of compromisers, recently I had an online exchange, via Fakebook, with someone who claims this culture that resides in my area. Now as I've stated, there isn't a high concentration of Five Percenters here so this creates an environment where either you're actually known, known of or completely unknown. If you're known then that's because you're out there doing community work, involved in publically recognized projects/programs and you're networking with various organizations and businesses. If you're known of then you're doing something that someone can/does vouch for. If you're unknown that's because you haven't made yourself (work) known for various reasons. Anyway, the person I had an exchange with is unknown in my area. Not because they don't know of me or have no way of getting in contact with me b.u.t. because they've chosen to be unknown for reasons known only to them. I guess today was their day to make contact.

The exchange started with her sending me a FB Message about how to figure out our Asiatic Calendar, inquiring about parliaments here and saying that she's gotten together with "The Queens" a couple of times here before but wasn't sure what's up with the rest of the cipher. Keep in mind that this

48

person is unknown in this area. Mentioning that I wasn't sure what degrees she actually knew by heart, I briefly explained how she can figure out our chronology on her own. She responded by saying that she's on the 2/1-14, that's why she needs a cipher and that, "I know ppl say ur 7 suppose to teach u but we work so much we are like two ships passing." Knowing that she is unknown and that if there are some Queens she'd be building with in this Area I would know them or know of them, I responded, "What Queens have you got together with, who is their educator and what degrees do they knowledge? As far as rallies/parliaments in Bethlehem I'm not aware of anyone organizing any. I'm more actively involved with the Five Percenters who're doing things in Steel City, Truth Cipher (Canada)."

She told me their names and both of them I'm aware of because they attended a few civilization classes and rallies I organized in my and her city before. While one has been around the lessons for years, because she was a student of a God I taught, the other started learning about who we are within the last five years. While the former has had a few different educators, I'm not sure what she actually knows and the other one has decided not to learn. Anyway, at this point in time both of them don't have an educator and it's unclear what lessons they have. In addition to them she mentions another female who has a righteous name on Facebook that's not worth mentioning. So now here's the picture... Three females getting together sometimes. The main one who contacted me has a God (Educator) and she says she's on the 2/1-14. The other two don't have an educator and it's unclear what lessons they have. All of them have righteous names, many friends on Facebook yet are unknown in this area.

At this point the female says she's trying to knowledge 120 by the Summer and not be around anybody that just don't care like that to which I respond, "I understand. We all invest time in what we cee as important and wherever we cee or don't cee going on in our area reflects our priorities. If that's your determined idea then you'll make it happen and put yourself in the position to be amongst those that care." At this point she said she mostly builds with one of the females who doesn't have an educator and she's been giving her lessons and "other degrees that pertain to Earths". She also added, "We figured we would just say f*ck it & teach each other." Hearing that she's still just a Newborn herself and not an educator, my response was, "What did your educator say in regards to giving someone lessons?" to which she responded, "I dont have one... never had one... I dont like to slow up somebody elses progress Cuz I maybe slow sometimes so I just gave it to her." This had me confused because she just said earlier that "I know ppl say ur 7 suppose to teach u but we work so much we are like two ships passing." Now this is where it really starts getting funny style...

Seeing what this situation could potentially be and not judging what the circumstances were surrounding her relationship/education I said, "So ya'll freestyling. I wouldn't suggest coming amongst us Five Percenters with a righteous name saying you have lessons, never had an educator and you're just giving lessons to somebody else." Instead of ceeing the wisdom in my words as a warning that it's not welcoming to come amongst Five Percenters calling yourself us when you clearly aren't, her response was, "Damn freestyling sounds like such a bad word for once. Hey im just being honest here." to which I responded, "That's definately not our tradition and is completely irresponsible." She goes on to ask, "What are we suppose to do now? Wait for someone to care?" and states that she's "had most since 07". Do you cee how complicated this is? Here's a person who says she's on the 2/1-14, her God ain't teaching her because they're both working, she don't have and never had an educator, she's teaching herself and giving some other female lessons and has had most for the last 5 years all in one FB message conversation..! What was my response having years of experience of ceeing this type of phenomenon? "Well for the last 5 years I think your approach/decisions already demonstrates you have your mind made up about what you want and how you want to do it. Most Five Percenters who learn about this won't trust your intentions or role you're striving to play within our nation since you haven't directly consulted us and chose to do your own thing. And if you're not upfront about what you told me exactly, you're even more suspect. Take a moment to read the post on my wall SciHonor Devotion tagged me in with the sword image. That will give you more insight into how that approach/decisions is perceived by many in our nation." Not only did I share with her my wisdom and experience b.u.t. I referred her to a source from a reputable Earth I know who gives her more clarity on the subject from a Woman's perspective. So instead of being receptive, this is what this female had to say before terminating our conversation, "Hold on your doing to much. I ain't never been suspect about nothing. Who is us? Just because I dont consult u dont mean I dont consult anyone... so ppls dont b confused. U know what nevermind. I was asking for help. Forget it."

My question to those of you reading this is: Does that seem like someone who's actually receptive to learn, seeking actual guidance and interested in true nation building? This is not me disqualifying anyone, I am simply pointing out how people disqualify themselves from having access to certain areas of growth and development because of their mouth, attitude, arrogance and rugged individualism. Remember the phrase

'Many shall come, only a few will be chosen and those who are chosen choose themselves'? Well this female, who obviously has some attraction to what we're doing in our nation, still hasn't chosen herself. Will she ever? That's not for me to say, it's her responsibility to get it together.

In the final analysis, it's all about our deeds. Even if people have had something to say negative about me I let time take care of them and eventually you've ceen their flames fade into some smoldering ashes of insignifigance -while I keep on doing what I've been doing; Building. It's not hard to recognize Who's Who amongst the Five Percent. Yeah some people may not be nationally known yet they are many who are very active, involved and known within their respective communities and regions, Five Percenters I'm grateful to have as family fulfilling our vision! This isn't hard to verify or substantiate, especially with the expansion of our online presence that documents our offline activities. This the reasoning behind my documentation and time stamping of some of the various things I do. It's about showing people this is really where I am, what I actually do and how I do it! My word or world ain't fake, staged, edited or surreal yet there's many people whose lives are fake, staged and edited to give others the appearance of something that doesn't exist. If I say I work out a certain amount of time I have the body to prove it. If I say I've published books I can refer you to a bookstore to order them. If I say I work with youth then they can tell you in their own words what our relationship is. All of us who are actually doing something to assist others in their growth and development and make our contribution to civilization adhere to these standards of integrity.

So in closing I emphasize the importance of our examination process. A process of inquiring who somebody's educator is, where they got their information, how long they had it and how they understand and are living what they have. This cultural tradition has allowed us, Five Percenters, to maintain a level of transparency and integrity within our nation since we formally began in 1964. WITHOUT this system of checks/balances there would be no way of determining Who's Who or even what "Who" is! Even though we may not all agree with one another all the time, we cannot deny eachothers work and contributions to our nation and society as a whole. For example, if you cee somebody who says they're from my area and you cee no interaction or actual contact between us then put two and two together. I'm out here; actively involved and have been available for years, months and days now. No these people don't have to be doing the exact same thing I'm doing b.u.t. there should be a level of social equality we have because we share the same common cultural cause right? A cause that I have taken the initiative to publically set and defend as an ever growing standard of our cultural integrity. If you're unsure about someone you're connected with on Facebook yet you cee they're in my area, ask me about them. If I say anything like, "I don't know them", "I met them before/once", "They contacted me on Facebook before" or "They came to 'a' civilization class" then put two and two together. This doesn't mean that I'm The Don or something. Lol I'm simply saying that I have some experience and success in the field of nation building, have established many relationships/networks and learn from others who are doing this and can tell you will confidence and surety who's involved in this -based upon their actions or lack thereof. These people may not be directly in my city b.u.t. I'm connected to Five Percenters within the surrounding areas and other regions who may/may not know them. I ran into an elder God out in Bethlehem one time who said he was from Pelon (the Bronx). As soon as I got the opportunity I reached out to another elder God (I-Freedom Born) in Pelon, who is his contemporary, to verify what this brother was telling me. Freedom was able to confirm everything all the way down to names and occupations of this God's siblings. Even though that all checked out it's still upon us to further examine a person's ways and actions. Sometimes people associate with others just to get a co-signer for their BS. Now imagine if these people aren't even connected to Five Percenters within the surrounding areas they live in, that also tells you something huh? Sometimes the cipher that's around them isn't progressive and they choose to not participate. That could be a legitimate reason for not coming around b.u.t. what are they doing about it? If all they're doing is going to work and claiming they're teaching their own babies, which isn't special because even animals are expected to perform this parental duty, it should raise an eyebrow about their ideas about real nation building... They may be playing the 'blame somebody else' game as an excuse to do the exact same thing they're accusing the cipher of doing; NOTHING. They also may just be people with a "me and mines!" mentality and they're using their child(ren) as a shield for their dirty, selfish religion. And if you do question them and hear the violins start to play as they give you this solicit for pity spiel about how they can't find nobody, maybe even for years and blah, blah, blah... even though myself and others are clearly right here, leave, them, alone. You've made knowledge born about your concerns and made yourself available to them if/when they're willing and able to "consistently" (key word!) add-on. They just need to work some things out first before they're ready to learn or finish what they started learning years ago.

Albert Pike 33 Degree
"One of the most influential American Freemasons"

Pike Dreams

This article is not an Albert Pike Expose, nor is it a trip down Illuminati Lane. This article is about the difference between advocating social justice vs. social status and knowing how to properly recognize the difference. I use Albert Pike as a model to illustrate this because his varied background provides a great social study for us to recognize these differences. The reasoning is to get us, especially black/brown people, to learn to think more critically about the sociopolitical platform of societies, organizations, fraternities, clubs, businesses and institutions before we join or become affiliated with them. To give you a basic backdrop of the social and political factors that played a significant role on in Albert Pike's life:

- He settled in Little Rock Arkansas in the early 1830's becoming a Teacher and Writer for the Arkansas Advocate Newspaper.
- He became the owner of the Advocate in 1835 and used it as a vehicle to promote views of the Whig Party that he was affiliated with. The Whig Party comes from the Scottish word *'whiggamore'* and were known as American Patriots, anti-Democratic and took many of the stances that would be considered 'far-right' today. The Whigs were succeeded by the Republican Party.
- He passed the Arkansas Bar in 1837 and became the first reporter of the Arkansas Supreme Court writing notes on points in court decisions, publishing and indexing the court's opinions. In 1842, he published the *Arkansas Form Book*, providing Lawyers with models for the different kinds of motions to be filed in the state's courts.
- He left the Whig Party because of their failure to take a unified pro-slavery stance. Pike then joined the Know Nothing Party.

The Know Nothing Party's platform was xenophobic (fear or dislike of foreigners/outsiders), anti-Catholic, against immigration/naturalization and often violent. This Party was considered semi-secret because members were instructed to reply, "I know nothing" If asked about the Party's activities. To join the Know Nothings you had to be a Protestant male born of British ancestry.

- In 1850 Pike became a Master Mason (Blue Lodge) at Western Star Lodge No. 2 in Little Rock, Arkansas. He received his York Rite (Red Lodge) degrees between 1850-1853. He received his Scottish Rite (Green Lodge) degrees in Charleston SC in 1853 from Albert G. Mackey. Pike received the 33rd degree on April 25, 1857 and was elected Sovereign Grand Commander of the Supreme Council of Scottish Rite's Southern Jurisdiction in 1859 and held that office for 32 years until his death. *Note the Red Lodge (York Rite) is a religious orientated wing of the Masonic Body and the Green Lodge (Scottish Rite) is a military orientated wing of the Masonic Body.

- Pike was pro-slavery and a Confederate General during the Civil War from 1861-1862. He supported succession from the Union and published a pamphlet in 1861 on that position titled *State or Province, Bond or Free?* In regards to acceptance of blacks as Masonic brothers, Pike was quoted as saying in a 1875 letter to his brother, "*took my obligation to White men, not to Negroes. When I have to accept Negroes as brothers or leave Masonry, I shall leave it."* (History and Evolution of Freemasonry 1954, page 329).

- Pike was said to be an active member of the Arkansas Branch of the Klu Klux Klan (KKK); a Movement founded in 1865 in Pulaski, TN by six Confederate ArmyVeterans. There are no public records of his involvement with the KKK. However, the book 'Ku Klux Klan', written by Walter Fleming (1905) states that Pike was the Chief Judicial Officer of the Klan. Also, the 'Authentic History Ku Klux Klan, 1865-77', written by Susan Lawrence Davis (1924) cites Pike as the Grand Dragon of the Klan for the state of Arkansas and Chief Judicial Officer appointed by Klan founder, Confederate General Nathan Bedford Forrest.

- From 1867-1868, Pike worked in Memphis, TN (about 4 hours away from Pulaski, TN) as editor of the Memphis Daily. He also established a new Law Partnership with Confederate General Charles W. Adams. In 1868 Pike wrote in the Tennessee Daily Appeal, *"With negroes for witnesses and jurors, the administration of justice becomes a blasphemous mockery. A Loyal League of negroes can cause any white man to be arrested, and can prove any charges it chooses to have made against him. The disenfranchised people of the South can find no protection for property, liberty or life, except in secret association. We would unite every white man in the South, who is opposed to negro suffrage, into one great Order of Southern Brotherhood, with an organization complete, active, vigorous, in which a few should execute the concentrated will of all, and whose very existence should be concealed from all but its members."*

- The Shriners, of which Pike is unkown to be a recorded Member, is a Masonic Body (founded in 1870) is not recognized as an appellant Masonic Body in the State of Arkansas. Prior to 2000, in order to join the Shriners aperson had to complete either the Scottish Rite and York Rite degrees of Masonry. Nowadays any Master Mason can join and they've streamlined Shrine Membership. William J. Simmons, founder of the 2nd Klu Klux Klan and Imperial Wizard was a Freemason and publisher of the KKK ritual handbook called the 'Kloran'.

- In 1871, Pike published the 900 + page Masonic handbook known as *Morals and Dogma of the Ancient andAccepted Scottish Rite of Freemasonry.* Although Pike published other Masonic works, Morals and Dogma is solidified Pike as the philosophical father of American Freemasonry to this day this book is traditionally given to many new initiates of a Masonic Lodge.

- By 1888, there were 7,210 Shriners in 48 Shrine Temples in the United States and Canada. Although the Shriners are said to not be connected to Islam and the Order originated from the imagination of Freemasons Physician Walter M. Fleming and Actor William J. Florence, in the "Former" History of the Imperial Council of Nobles of the Mystic Shrine it states that "the

Order of Nobles of the Mystic Shrine was instituted by the Caliph Ali in 656 AD" (Page 36-40).

- Pike is still the only Confederate General to have an outdoor statue displayed in Washington, D.C. and the statue is at Judiciary Square.

Since a picture is worth a thousand words, do these images/symbols associated with Albert Pike's legacy make sociopolitical sense?

Original Ku Klux Klan Costume (notice the star and crescent)

Original Ku Klux Klan Costume (notice the star and crescent)

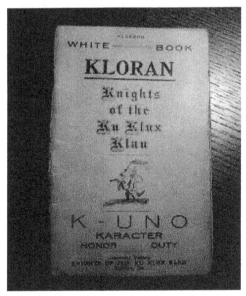

Ritual Book written by KKK Grand Wizard/Freemason William J. Simmons ('Kloran' is a play on the Islamic word 'Koran/Quran')

KLAN ORGANIZED IN ROLFE

We have been reliably informed that a klan of the Klu Klux has been organized in Rolfe with the following officers:

Exalted Cyclops—vbgkqj cmfwyp
Klaliff— etaoin shrdlu.
Klokard— xzfififf etaoin.
Kludd—cmfwyp shrdlu.
Klabee—123456 7890$.
Kligrapp—cmfwyp vbgkqj.
Kladd— etaoin ahrdlu.
Klarogo—xzfififf vbgkqj.
Klexter—vbgkqj cmfwyp.
Klokan—bgkqj etaoin.
Klokann—xzfifl vbgk cmwf.
Night Hawk—shrdlpywfm nloate.
Kleagle—R. A. N. K. Outsider.

The courtesies of The Arrow have been extended to every secret society or order in Rolfe. From time to time we have published the full list of of-

KKK Language (notice word 'Klaliff' is a play on the Islamic word Khalif/Caliph)

Image of a Shriner (notice the word Islam, star and crescent)

Shriner Patch (notice the Freemasonic square and compass where the star usually goes)

Racoons, known for being "tricksters", were the early symbol of the Whig Party. The racoon also symbolize being "frontiersman" (pioneering colonialists)

Know Nothing Party Flag (Native Americans referred to "Native-born White Citizens")

Confederate Flag (symbol for the South who were pro-slavery)

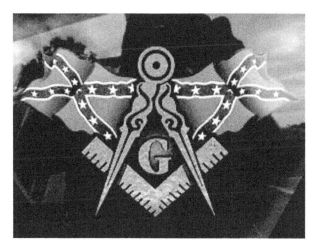

Confederate Flag/Masonic Decal (Pike was a Confederate Army General and 33 Degree Freemason)

Symbol of the Scottish Rite. Latin for "My Hope is in God". The two-headed eagle symbolizes guarding it's agenda in the East and West. Pike was Sovereign Grand Commander of the Supreme Council for 32 years.

The Scottish Rite Southern Jurisdiction's Supreme Council Headquarters in Washington DC

Scottish Rite Temple dedicated to Pike on the US National Historic Registry

Albert Pike Memorial in Washington DC

Contrary to what many people would like us to believe about Albert Pike, he was far from double-headed and his affiliations/views were consistent throughtout his lifetime. Now, upon closer examination of Albert Pike's colorful legacy and affiliations what does this tell you about his sociopolitical worldview? Can you say that the allegiances he forged and partnerships he formed were for social justice or a social status (quo)? More importantly, are the allegiances we forge and partnerships we form for social justice or a social status (quo)?

"When you look at an organization with so many members at the top of the socioeconomic food chain, in so many industries, do you NOT THINK they'll do whatever is necessary to put mechanisms in place to protect their group interests, its members and maintain their status quo?" -Life

I received an anonymous email the other day from a 'Jane Doe' who asked me, "Can Gods and Earths become Freemasons?" My response to her, if it was a her, was that people can choose to do whatever they want yet the question is what is their reasoning for those decisions and are they Right & Exact? If a God/Earth is truly invested and committed to our common cause and recognizes that 'God' or 'Earth' is the apex of their identity, there is no need to 'become' anything else. I'm not saying that we shouldn't forge alliances with others. It's important for others to add-on with us and to share a common cause as long as it doesn't fundamentally compromise 'What We Teach' or 'What We Will Achieve' as a nation. Unfortunately, there are alot of gate keepers; people and groups that are only interested in maintaining and upholding the status quo, not true social justice. So for us to claim a sense of social justice and simultaneously join or affiliate ourselves people and societies, organizations, fraternities, clubs, businesses and institutions that are maintainers of the status quo it neutralizes us from bringing about any effective change. Especially when they're 'special interest groups' we as black/brown people didn't have a voice in founding or don't have a voice in modifying their mission statement. Albert Pike was a man of many faces. Yet when you look at his affiliations and the social and political factors that played a significant role in his life, you'll cee what his determined idea was. Obviously all of these political parties, societies and good ole boy networks provided common, consistent resources for him. If not, he couldn't have used them, he wouldn't have been involved in them, nor would there be any traces of his affiliation. Among other things, this article shows you that being a white protestant, Freemason, Shriner, Confederate, anti-immigrationist Klansman is not contradictory and there's obviously a place in all of these white special interests groups for someone who has these views to flourish and prosper... This article also shows that there are built in mechanisms in place that will undermine, neutralize and dismantle any progress towards true social justice because that was never the objective of some of these white special interests groups from the beginning. I say "some" because Freemasonry (and Shriners) was established for the purpose of raising upright men (and women who belong to masonic bodies). Yet like one 33 degree white mason/shriner once told me directly, "In the 32 years I've been a mason there is only one flaw that I've found. It's made up of human beings and you can never say what you'll do in a given situation!" So after all this conversation about Freemasonry making good men better and how the working tools help build a perfected man he not only tells me how human "they" are and how "they" will fall short b.u.t. how they ultimately accept these falls/flaws as a part of who "they" are. (9, 10/1-14) That sounds like "hug your imperfections", "proceed with caution" or worst yet "enter at your own risk" to me; not very encouraging when it comes to a trustworthy relationship where you can depend on someone to do the right thing when situations get rough. As Five Percenters we strive for perfection and don't settle for mediocracy, especially when it comes down to doing the right thing. Culturally speaking, that weak posture and attitude contradicts (destroys) what's divine. Our stance is "we are just and true and there is no unrighteousness in us" because we are committed to "show forth our power that we are allwise and righteous... WITHOUT FALLING VICTIM TO the devils civilization" (37, 38/1-40). So regardless how rough situations get, we're determined to seek the right way and trick-knowledge, devilishment, stealing, telling lies or mastering others is never an acceptable option (4/1-14). I've ceen and heard people make the argument that, "they had to do what they had to do" or "the ends justify the means" when in reality they're simply confirming that they don't really recognize righteousness as the ultimate standard to adhere to "regardless to whom or what" (11/1-14). In otherwords, they're still NOT CONVINCED that righteousness is infallible (unfailing) and that there's always a right way to act or respond in any given situation. That is a tragedy for them and will be tragic for anyone around them whenever these people feel like situations are getting too rough...

In closing, I ask all of us, regardless if we call ourselves Five Percenters [Gods/Earths], Moors, Hebrews, Muslims, Kemetians, Nuuwabians or etc., are we truly seeking social justice or a social status? Are we like the double-headed eagle of the Scottish Rite; claiming we're about social justice (revealing the truth to all who seek it) yet simultaneously upholding the status quo (concealing the truth from the uninitiated)? Many of the special interest groups many of you are intrigued about joining don't even offer you the benefit of full disclosure and transparency about what you'd be committing your life/finances to upfront! For you to even be interested in that means that you either have done or can cee yourself doing the same thing; there's an affinity for the 10%. Committing yourself to something under these clandestine circumstances is like agreeing to marry somebody you don't really know and who's not allowed to tell you much about themselves until you say "I do!" Regardless of how great they say they are, the benefits you'll get from the relationship and etc., the very foundation is untrustworthy and unequal. You have no way of judging whether that's true or not and you're completely vulnerable (open) to what they need to get from you. In otherwords, there is nothing restricting you from sharing everything about yourself with them yet they're restricted from sharing everything equally with you. It reminds me of those who 'petition' to join a lodge or go 'on-line' for fraternities/sororities; there's a thorough investigation done on you yet you have limited resources to actually investigate its members or the group you want to join... Then if they do decide to let you in, you're required to uphold the same standard. If anything, it says alot about a person's self esteem and social ambitions to put themselves in that position to begin with. Nobody who is truly concerned about social injustice would put themselves in such an unjust position.

So for those of you who're truly about real social justice, be mindful of joining or affiliating yourselves with anything that serves the purpose of neutralizing your efforts. If you've already made decisions like this and now you cee those societies, organizations, fraternities, clubs, businesses and Institutions undermine your ability to work towards social justice then you have a serious choice to make! And when I say undermine your ability to work towards social justice, it can be anything from paying dues to them that could otherwise go towards something else or even actively attending their events that create conflicts in your schedule for participating in our events. Some of you will dismiss this article by simply saying you only joined or are affiliating yourselves with certain societies, organizations, fraternities, clubs, businesses and institutions to preserve the best part for yourselves and add-on to your foundation. What you really mean is you're trying to climb the social ladder, seek upward mobility or get a piece of the American Pie. My questions to you are, "Whose ladder?" Up to where? Who's pie? Others will even go as far as to say that some special interest groups aren't keepers of the status quo. I've heard Prince Hall Freemasons claim that they're independent from England and American Grand Lodges so they're not keepers of the status quo yet when I ask them, "Who gave them permission (their charter/quo), Where is this charter kept in a vault, Where is the cornerstone of their original lodge said to be kept and does all of this reflect true self determination and autonomy for us as a people?" they don't have any answers. Well I'll leave all of you with this thought: If your involvement and participation in something is clearly keeping you apart from "our own social equality", then that ultimately reveals where your allegiance lies. And to believe otherwise is nothing but a Pike Dream. (8/1-14) For those of you who already know what's up, I appreciate the work you're doing to continually advocate true social justice. The Father (Allah) and other men and women who demonstrated this unwavered integrity couldn't be bought or sold! And it was because of this commitment to our common cause that we are here today.

Cryptic Codes

"*Audio files and file cabinets by the Patmos Isles/swimming the Nile with Peter Wolf and his two exotic rooks/cooking sundials/creating secret potions of an ageless child/out last the time avalanches and Quahadi dances.../through a ceremony and Seracean demeanors/see what I mean?/see what I'm meaning?*" - (Cryptic Codes)

Over the years with the expansion of the internet and social networking, I've learned more and more how important it is to not take for granted what someone knows or what they've been exposed to when I'm striving to communicate my ideas. As a Journalist I've also learned as a rule of thumb "*don't assume or take for granted where others are in their growth & development and be specific in regards to the audience I'm targeting.*" In many of my articles you've noticed that I often put a numerical reference at the end of the sentence. This is specifically done for Five Percenters who have those cultural references so they recognize exactly where I'm coming from.

Because I'm usually not writing/speaking to the general public in our pure language, I've been able to target a much larger audience who're sincerely striving to grow and develop.

People reach out to me from all over the world all the time about how easy to understand I make the principles/values within my culture and I really appreciate that! It's just confirmation for me that I'm communicating effectively. People also reach out to me and raise questions about what I've written/said and often ask me to elaborate further on something I may have only mentioned or didn't mention at all. I also appreciate this because these sincere exchanges help me learn to communicate even more effectively.

"We can't give someone understanding; they have to cee things for themselves. What we can and are responsible for giving them is the best opportunity to understand and for us to be understood, and this is done through effective communication."

As Five Percenters, our language can be very cryptic and abstract, not only to an outsider b.u.t. even to those within our nation depending upon how they were taught and their exposure to other Five Percenters. We are not a monolithic group. There are some I know personally who are directly involved in their city's local/regional politics while there are others who wouldn't touch politics with a ten foot pole. There are Gods I know that say it's all (and sometimes only) about Supreme Mathematics while negating the importance of memorizing 120 lessons while other Gods will tell you strait up that 120 is the Foundation. There are Earths who know little to nothing about 120 and others who know, speak and understand 120 better than alot of Gods. So just within our nation alone there is a wide range of perspectives; some culturally based, others that aren't culturally based, and can poise various challenges towards effective communication and coming to a cultural/national consensus. This is WITHIN our cipher. Now imagine the communication challenges that exist with those who are clearly on the OUTSIDE of our nation... Consider what it takes to come to a consensus with someone who really doesn't know about or hasn't been exposed to your culture. Even if they have been exposed to something or know of something they came across on the Internet or even books, that poises an initial challenge of finding out what that exposure was, how much they were exposed to and if that exposure was the right or wrong perspective. I've had experiences with people reaching out to me about learning our culture and when I asked them about what they've been exposed to, just their honorable mention of some people's names told me what type of job I would have in store for me if I decided to educate them. See, many of us are under the impression that "building" is all about telling others what we think. I think we're more effective listening to what others know and what they've been exposed to first. Then we can more accurately determine what their needs are and if we're even capable of meeting those needs.

Just because someone asks for something, especially something that is culturally sacred (such as Supreme Mathematics, Supreme Alphabet and 120 lessons) doesn't mean that we should give it to them. 95% of the time (85% + 10%) they don't even know what they're asking for! Instead of just handing them Supreme Mathematics (with your name on it!) or even lessons, stop for a moment and ask, "What is the reason for learning?" You may be floored by their response. So it's best to find out up front if this person is really sincere about growth & development, only interested in boosting their lyrics, getting a man or using your righteous name to shield their dirty religion. Some people literally approach learning our culture like you're hittin' 'em off with a lick. They usually have no idea that "the knowledge" they're asking for is really a lifelong relationship that's based upon our commitment to improve ourselves, others and our environment. One time I asked a dude, "What's the reason you want to learn?" and he said, "It's like, I'm just striving to get that money and I'm going to get it regardless!" I've also had other experiences with people sniffing around wanting to learn and if I didn't invest the time to find out what they knew and had been exposed to I would have ended up "deputizing" undercover active Knights Templars or Pan-Hellenics.

In closing, I cannot stress enough the importance of effective communication. When we don't invest the time to find out what others know, don't know, have been exposed to or haven't been exposed to BEFORE we start communicating where ew're coming from we always run the risk of leaving them to their own devices. In otherwords, don't assume or take for granted that others have an understanding of the word 'freedom' the way you undestand it. You may be using the word 'freedom' in relationship to cultural development and they may think you mean "Doowutchyalike" (Do What You Like!). The so-called intellectuals or 'people who study everything' might think you're saying we need to be more like "Caligula." The next thing you know this person walks away from a whole conversation you had with them about 'freedom' and now they're confidently sharing their hedonistic ideas with others with your name attached to it... The bottom line is this: *Just because someone nods their head and keeps their mouth shut it doesn't mean they understand or agree with what you're saying.* You won't know for sure where a person's head is at or how they're processing the information you're sharing with them until you simply ask them. Ask them how they cee what you're saying and ask them to explain what you're saying in their own words. You'll both be learning because they may raise some questions or point out more effective ways that you can communicate. This way you're giving them the best opportunity to understand and for you to be understood. That's indeed equality and the premise upon which effective communication and harmonious relationships must be built. If not, there will be obvious inequalities and comprehension gaps. If something is important enough to us to share with others.., then it's also important enough for us to do our best to share it.

Lupe Fiasco

Lupe Fiasco for President!
-*A Message to the Voters/Non-Voters*-

With candidates gearing up for the 2016 Presidential Election I've come in contact with many people who don't vote and aren't involved in the political process. Cool. I definately understand how they think. What I don't agree with is the apathy that accompanies non participation. In otherwords, although they

84

can give you a laundry list of reasons why they don't Vote and aren't involved in the political process, rarely do they share even a few concrete, practical alternatives to not voting or not being involved in the political process. It always leaves me wondering just how much thought they really put into politics and the political process itself. It also leaves me wondering about their concern for the many people who actually share their sentiments... Without having any concrete, practical alternatives to an ideology, program or political structure we don't support, we consequently support that ideology, program or political structure by default. For example, if we don't support public schools because we claim they suppor the misducation of our youth yet aren't providing viable alternatives such as charter schools, homeschooling, GED programs and etc., then we're apathetically supporting the same system of miseducation we accuse the public schools of promoting because we ourselves have nothing to offer. Therefore, the youth are left to stay in public school or drop out and fend for themselves. I can't speak for you b.u.t. I don't think those are very good alternatives.

The above paragraph exemplifies a common non-participatory approach I cee many people take towards 'unsolving' the problems we face. We often have a various creative ways of critiquing problems, pointing out flaws and articulating why we aren't going to support something yet invest little thought, time, finances and etc. in providing actual solutions. The next time you hear somebody explaining why they don't do something or support a certain program, ask them, "What's your suggestion as an alternative?" More often than not, you and they'll be surprised what they actually come up with. What you will find, in most cases, is that they never even put much thought into doing something about it beyond words. This sheds light on a greater problem than the ones you heard them pointing out in the first place.

One of the lessons I've learned growing up and that was reinforced through gaining Knowledge of Self is that it's not enough to point out a problem without striving to provide a solution. Growing up in a household with six siblings we were all responsible for taking responsibility and playing our part. There was always work to do and playing the 'blame sombody else' game didn't allow us to get the work done. Yes we tried and were usually unsuccessful. In order for our family to operate with some basic level of efficiency we all had to pitch in and help -whether that was doing dishes, dusting or have a sock party (where we'd all sit down and match the washed socks). Likewise, in order for our communities, cities, counties, regions and states to operate with some basic level of efficiency we all have to pitch in and help too. My siblings and I weren't allowed to get away with pointing out a problem and not striving to do something about it or not being held accountable for helping solve it. I couldn't imagine my Ole Earth or Ole Dad running around to put out brush fires, and there were alot, everytime one of us ran to them about a problem. Wisely they delegated responsibility to us by age and taught us to develop problem solving skills to address these issues ourselves. I'm thankful I got it and learned to further develop this strategy towards Life as I've grown and developed. I'm sure that many of us didn't grow up in this way and possibly the 'blame somebody else game' was a way of life in our household, yet that doesn't sentence us to a life of irresponsibility. As Adults we have a choice and if a philosophy or approach towards Life isn't working out for us we have the power to change that.

I would like to make a few suggestions to those of us who aren't voting in the upcoming Presidential Election or who aren't involved in the poltitical process as a whole. First and foremost it's important to recognize that your non-participation makes you an unwilling participant by default. You're still subject to all of the governmental policies and procedures that are enforced on a national, regional and local level. To simply choose to have no say (voice) or opt out in how these policies and procedures are drafted, implemented and enforced on a national, regional and local level doesn't mean that you, your family, your community and your place of employment won't be affected by these policies and procedures. As a matter of fact, to choose to have no say (voice) translates into your 100% approval. If we don't approve then surely we should be willing and able to provide some concrete, practical alternatives that we approve through participation. If we haven't come up with anything we actually do or we can encourage others to do, then we're doing ourselves and others an injustice by having nothing to offer b.u.t. words. Keep in mind that if it really came down to it people will drink mop water if there's nothing there for them to drink... So this is what I suggest to those who don't Vote or aren't involved in the political process:

1.) Do something about it. If you're not voting or involving yourself in the political process then come up with some practical alternatives. When I say "practical alternatives" I'm talking about concrete activities people can engage in right now that will help empower them in a way that government is supposed to. I'm talking about practices that can be implemented amongst those who share the same sentiments on a daily basis that serves the needs of the people. If you don't agree with the governmental policies towards funding arts programs then do something about it by establishing an arts program or committing yourself to helping financially support arts programs.

2.) Network with those who share your sentiments. Network doesn't mean get together and vent, trade conspiracy theories or beat up on Fox News about what's going on in this society. You're intelligence and their intelligence equals a whole lot of intellectual compacity to either change the system as we know it or set up your own. If that's not the reasoning or goal for why you're congregating with eachother then what's the point? Personally I and many others may agree with many of your thoughts about politics and the poltitical process b.u.t. simply because we got together and didn't do anything above and beyond talking, we feel no more inspired, educated or empowered about the future than before we met.

3.) If you're not actually doing anything about it then save your time and breath. I didn't say "going to do" something, I specifically said "doing" something. In my short lifetime I've been to many meetings to meet about something to plan another meeting about what we need to meet about. Years, months and days later nothing has changed and the same concerns exist. A simple rule I've learned to follow is that if I don't have anything to offer than I don't have anything to offer. Make sense? In otherwords, if I'm not in the position where I know for a fact that I can get someone employed, I'm not going to have a long discussion about how a person needs to stop hustling or sitting around not working. Usually THE FIRST THING people who are in positions will say is, "I don't have a choice" (there aren't any alternatives). And if you can't provide any alternatives then you are simply a part of the problem. I know you mean well and don't cee yourself that way b.u.t. that's what you actually are. Hey, you may be able to get them a job at Burger King which ain't equal to the paper they make on the block b.u.t. at least it's some thing. Something they probably won't have to always look over their shoulder, over the counter or through the drive thru to do. If anything, they'll at least recognize that you cared enough to provide an alternative for them beyond a mini lecture and you never know, they may follow you up on that!

In closing I just wnat to emphasize the importance of being proactive. Regardless if you choose to vote and be involved in the political process or not, we all need to play a positive and productive role in our families and places where we live (communities) to ensure that it's a better place for us, our children and our elders. There are many things we share in common and take a vested interest in regardless of our political or non-political stances and it often takes a shift in our geopolitical landscape (Hurricane Sandy) to cee this and work together. So regardless who gets elected as the President of the United States, let us at least agree to commit ourselves to being Presidential in our families and communities. Let us at the very least agree to take more responsibility and be accountable for the change we desire to cee, not simply in words but in deeds!

The 30th Annual Family Day in Power Hill (Philadelphia)
I-Freedom Born, Divine Universal, C'BS ALife, Lord Life Justice, Unikue Thorough and Justice Understanding

The Fossil Phrase Phenomenon

The idea of "Fossil Phrases" came to me one day when I was commenting on one of Facebook friend's status. She mentioned the phrase "old heads" and it struck a chord because I'm not used to hearing some of the younger generation using phrases like that. Not to say I'm an "old head", b.u.t. many of the younger generation I directly or indirectly come in contact with are more prone to use phrases like "I ain't even trying to hear that" and "I ain't feelin' that" to describe their relationship with the older generation; which are nothing more than 'mute buttons' for the advice an "old head" or anyone is striving to share with them. Heck, there are many people my 'physical degree' (age) and older following suit! The fact that this young woman even used this phrase says volumes about her principles, values and family dynamics as a whole... It was refreshing. Refreshing enough to write a whole article about the fossilization of phrases.

When I was coming of age there were various different phrases, lingo, proverbs we used to describe and define where we are at and how we were living. Some of these phrases, like "That's cold blooded!" were recognized nationally while there were other cryptic phrases like, "I'm going to the office", that were locally understood amongst my peers. Regardless if these phrases were national, regional or local they all served the same purpose; psychologically and socioeconomically orientating us. For example, "I can't call it" was never a response me and my companions used when someone asked us, "What's going on?" We had an answer, even if it was negative, we at least knew what to call it. A couple generations before me, because of the socioeconomic climate, the answer to "What's going on?" would have been a variation of "revolution." I think that as long as we're continuing to at least ask eachother, "What's going on?" there's always going to be an opportunity to consider where we are at, how we are livin' AND what is actually going on.

Anytime a people elevated their condition, whether from a primative state to a level of civilization or from a menial position to that of entreprenuer, they had to undergoe a process to reorientate themselves psychologically and socioeconomically. Within this reorientation process came a change in the way they communicate; how they define, describe themselves and also process data communicated to them from the World. In otherwords, elevation was made possible on one condition, that a person grow! In the bible it talks about being as a child and speaking as a child and when we grew to become a man (or woman) we put childish things away. Well our commitment towards growth & development is always apparent in the what/how we communicate, whether that's through our words or ways. It is my position that the fossilization of certain phrases that convyed important principles, values and reinforced positive family dynamics for us as a people is one of the reasons why many of our present generation "can't call it"...

One of the most interesting things about The Nation of Gods and Earths (Five Percenters) is that since our inception we've taken a direct approach towards reorientating people, particularly the youth, via a cultural worldview that codified a unique language, phrases, lingo and proverbal wisdom to transit/receive principles, values and reinforce positive family dynamics that elevate our condition. We, like many of our Ancestors at various times and in various different geographic locations, recognized a need for people to grow & development and take responsiblity for aiding others in their growth & development. And for these relationships to be resourceful, sustainable, and perpetuated, there had to be a language to hold these bonds together. So within our language we don't say, "What's up?" to one another. We simply say "Peace". It's the way we greet eachother and the way we depart. A common phrase we also use is, "What's the science?" This basically means, "What are you aware of, what do you know or what are you studying/learning about life right now?" This way of communicating with eachother demands not only a level of responsibility/accountability for what we're doing in our lives and for eachother b.u.t. it also communicates that our Worldview is rooted in reinforcing critical analytical thinking skills. If a Five Percenter were to ask another Five Percenter "What's the science?" and they replied, "Nothing" or didn't have a legitimate explanation for what they're doing in their life that's the first sign that they're "stagnating" <----- as we call it, which means "they're dull, inactive and not growing"; the complete opposite of what our way of life is based upon. Although the concepts we hold fast to and language we use to convey/reinforce them about how we should treat one another, our relationship to nature, dietary/healthcare choices and etc.

are ancient (classical), we express many of these concepts in a contemporary context. For example, the ancient proverbial wisdom, "If you are a person who judges, listen carefully to the speech of one who pleads." would be communicated in our language as, "When you do the knowledge to the cipher that's Just I cee equality." So in comparison to the ancient proverbial wisdom we actually take it a step further by informing someone that "getting to know a person, place or thing is the basis for us being able to treat that person, place or thing fairly". Of course this only explains what that means on the surface and there are many deeper meanings to the phrase, "When you do the knowledge to the cipher that's Just I cee equality." If I translated that phrase numerically (in a mathematical equation) all I simply said was, "1 + 0 = 10". Alphabetically? Justice. It's pretty sophisticated and isn't a language and way of living a person can thoroughly grasp by remote viewing it. In my articles, videos and books I strive to translate our cultural concepts and communicate them in the everyday language of the layperson. Some things I can, many things I can't; because a person would have to live this culture, oftentimes for a substantial number of years, before they're able to understand many things.

Over the years people have always been intrigued, interested and attracted to the sophisticated way we communicate with one another and how we describe/define the world. What many fail to realize, even those who have personally studied our culture through an enlightener, is that the language, phrases, lingo and proverbal wisdom we use aren't "fossil phrases". They're not out of date, antiquated nor do they 'belong' to the past. I say this because even within our culture there are certain phrases, lingo and proverbal wisdom that was shared by our "Old Heads" that some of the present date Five Percenters don't use anymore. For example, the phrase, "science it up" which was commonly used in the 1970's is rarely used today. With the present day backdrop of pseudoscience, ghetto scholarship and Illuminatiology paraded around on the Internet and through the media, the phrase "science it up" would do alot to help our present generation to stay rooted in and reinforce their critical analytical thinking skills. The fossilization of valuable phrases such as this can only mean one of two things A.) "I can't call it." or B.) The younger generation must create contemporary phrases that reflect ancient concepts. Regardless if it's A. or B. both of them point to our responsibility/accountability as adults to assist them in the process. Even if that means refusing to respond to them in a language that promotes stagnation b.u.t. being wise enough to offer them a fly alternative. I mention that because I know/talk to alot of adults who cringe and complain when they hear the youth saying "Nigga" or other colorful words/phrases yet they don't even offer them an alternative attractive enough to make then even consider changing their language. This is why many of the youth "aren't even trying" to hear that...

In the Nation of Gods and Earths we have a commone phrase that says, "We preserve the best part and don't care about the poor part." When it comes to those various different phrases, lingo and proverbial wisdom that's a fundamental part of communicating our principles, values and reinforcing positive family dynamics, it's important to preserve them. They are the best part! It is likewise important to not show interest or desire in perpetuating those things that stagnate us. That is the poor part and it only keeps us in a state of moral, intellectual and physiological poverty. There are many phrases that are fossils and should remain as such yet there are many others that should have never been treated like a fad. To better distinguish the best from the poor part start consulting with old heads. Ask them about phrases we used and what they meant they'll 'make knowledge born' ('make knowledge born' is a phrase that basically means "to make it known so a person will be equipped with the proper information to change their situation"). Regardless if they know the difference themselves, they'll at least be able to give you information so you can do further research and distinguish it for yourself.

Original Cover Design by Otis 'Blaqlion' Arterberry III

Experiments with High Explosives

-TheChronicles of a 'Big Headed' Scientist-

This is an excerpt from "**Journal Log Entry #4 (*...mist which the naked eye could hardly detect...*).**" It's a candid Conversation between Ramadyn and True Equality about one of their God brothers named 'Just' who's alittle naive when it comes to women.

"Yo it's funny you ask that though. Me and Just was building this morning and I don't know if he built with you yet b.u.t. he wanted you to build with Cee Wisdom."

"You mean 'Ya-Ya' God?" she said sarcastically. "You know that ain't right Queen" I said laughing.

"What God?! I told Just a loooong time ago that 'Ya-Ya' would always be 67 million miles away from the Sun. Just seems to believe he can 'make' Earth so what can I do about that?" True Equality said while shruggin' her shoulders. She continued, "If I went over there and tried to build with that female about mathematics she'll act like I'm tryin' to cause trouble amongst her and Just and strive to have us tryin' to fight and kill one another. All I'll do is tell the God what I told him from the door; You can't make a 'Ho' into no 'Home' of Islam!"

"You, are, off, the, hook, Queen! Be nice Queen" I said, holding my stomach in laughter.

"I told Just that without 'me' meaning 'what I stand for as a black woman' all you get is a 'Ho' and half a 'Home'! Word is bond God, it got me heated just thinking about how he got that destroy power chick over his rest like that knowing that the only thing

100

she sincerely love is his divine eye and the cream he be giving her!

This is an excerpt from "**Journal Log Entry #7 (*...its high speed of rotating makes it impossible.*)**." Ramadyn is pondering his loneliness and lack of intimacy while sharing his feelings about coming to terms with some life changing information he just received. It's an island abyss where sometimes you can't even depend upon the sanity of your own thoughts.

Dealing with the lack of intimacy in my life at that time was like trying to kick a heroin addiction. Many nights I tossed and turned in my bed visualizing Divinity and wishing that she were lying beside me. On a few occasions I'd have a fling b.u.t. I'd always come back to my senses. Messing around never filled the emptiness I felt inside and these quasi- relationships always ended as abruptly as they'd began. I just couldn't keep consummating situations that my Heart wasn't in.

Cee, one twenty is a 'map' that only infers the emotional 'terrain' of our two forty and we get the understanding of this wilderness by ourselves. Many Gods methodically quote one hundred twenty degrees b.u.t. I learned to live one hundred and twenty lessons. I've felt the subtle mist never drawn above six in the pit of my stomach. I experienced the joy of ceeing the planet first founded and I recognize the expression of a baby being fed the wrong foods. True Gods and Earths stand to be corrected about this 'map' and add on knowledge about its 'terrain'. Although I added on what True Equality dropped on me, that knowledge locked me in a seat of an emotional rollercoaster; a ride I had to have the stomach for regardless of whom or what! I had to respect True Equality for not making knowledge born to me sooner because I definitely wouldn't have had the strength to deal with hearing about Divinity.

I went from feeling angry, frustrated, sad, jealous to strait up dumb at a terrific speed and there were still painful questions swirling around in my Third. I was nowhere near 20 miles outside of this situation and being a Scientist was the last thing on my Mind. At that moment I was nothing b.u.t. a hopeless romantic, caught up in my emotions and ready to mount a crusade to save the Queen from a burning castle.

As True Equality left my rest I could feel myself slowly sinking into a deep, dark, pit of loneliness. I really needed a God to build with so I could restore my self esteem and gain my Godly perspective back. True Equality's words felt like daggers piercing my Heart and my feelings for Divinity had me doubting who I was.

Below are some excerpts from my book "The Beholder; a Book of Poetry, Prose and Philosophy"

The Beholder

The World in all its majesties is never as mysterious as we assume it to be. Even though our heart is at times unrevealed and the weight of our words & actions undefined, the truth will eventually be unveiled. We are the truth in which we seek.

Many people's concept of righteousness is NOT GETTING CAUGHT!

Life and Living

Your Life is the source of many inspirational insights! You may be a single mother with 3 children, someone working as a bartender, you breed cats, you traveled to Hawaii, you were in prison 5 Years, you make a living teaching singing lessons, maybe you're in Coast Guard or etc. Always keep in mind that what you may take for granted is an amazing story/experience to someone else! Sharing your life is living.

The Dream Dreams The Dreamer

I never believed that each person is predisposed to any given station in life. To look back at our life along with all its variables, each person would see a perfectly written script from Incarnation to wherever they presently stand. Even the most chaotic experiences will began to make perfect sense. As we gaze into our future we will see an inkless tablet, yet it is solely our responsibility to decide who, why, when, where and how that script shall be written.

Relativity...

One thing that's common between many religions/cultures is that their most fundamental and significant relationship is between God and Earth; creator and creation. It is through this sacred bond that forces of nature nurtures life!

Try Knowledge of Self! I promise to give you a full refund on your ignorance if it doesn't work.

Sankofa

Met on an unassuming Sunday
She was wrapped in a way to tickle Allah's attention
Did the knowledge from afar with Cliff Notes and Godly radar
The science was '6' b.u.t. high explosive experiments
She was slick, moved just within an earshot to smuggle some of the Math I got
I stopped and let the newborn who build a lot, add-on to keep the cipher warm, word is bond and bond is life

I cee you and you cee me
There was no lie between our eyes
You front like you can't cee

The truth became revealed when your thoughts went into motion

You're celestial like a Planet and smooth like aloe vera lotion

Time and Space is of no relevance within my dimension

Didn't mention who I am 'cuz you ain't ready

Keep it steady as I aim for your heart

I paint your desires like it's art

Just like your picture

Fulfilled your scripture

Descended in your realm when I met you, also brought form the jewels of Life I casted like a spell...

I swell your Mind with the things I cee, and say

Your innocent play and determined ideas I mode like clay

We are the Future

The Past and this Present Life

My Kingdom needs a Queen and on the Earth a Wife

When my Mind detects your feelings, vibrations of your emotions

Don't restrict your perception, my body's just a vehicle my mental plane just coasts in

Transcend my physical form, keep your thoughts warm in a dark womb in your Mind

The blind don't know exist

Reality is fixed

My understanding distills in the form but my ideas remain a

mist

Cee all things are added unto you

I'll build a way of life around you to support you

Racism

One of the worst kinds of racist are those environmentalists and conservationists that spend millions of dollars going all out to save plant/animal life yet won't spend a dime to save the endangered lives of indigenous (first world) people and their descendants -the original environmentalists who successfully conserved this planet for millions of years before they got here.

Parenting; L.I.E.U.T.E.N.A.N.T.

"The duty of the Lieutenant is to 'teach' and also 'train' the Private Soldier" (13/1-14)

One thing about my parents they never co-signed or ignored anything they thought wasn't right and exact. At times they'd bomb me and my siblings about something or walk us through the reason and logic of something so we can cee it for ourselves. When I was in high school one time the police came to my house looking for one of my brothers. My Ole Earth and I were sitting on the front porch when they walked up. They humbly asked my Ole Earth was he here and she said, "Oh yeah, he's right inside." Next thing you know they were escorting my brother out of the house and he had this "Save Me!" look on his face. What was my Ole Earth's response? She looked dead at him, turned her head and started to sing 'Gangsta Lean' (*"this is dedicated to my homies..."*) and started to pour her coffee out on the porch like a libation. I, was, horrified! I could not believe that she could be so heartless and unaffected by the police taking my brother, her child, away and it took me years to understand her logic. I cried and was angry all at the same time. I was upset and brother was going to jail and I was upset my Ole Earth sat back and didn't do anything about it, in fact, she clowned him.

This story haunted me until I had my own children and became a parent myself. As a parent, I learned that there were strategies to raising children and that as they grew older I had to update many of these strategies to better address their needs. Reflecting back on my brother being taken away, that was his own doing. My Ole Earth had consistently talked to him about various choices he was making and her words couldn't stop him. Unfortunately, he had to put his own theories to the test and found out for himself that there wasn't a right way to do wrong. My Ole Earth was simply wise enough to not get in the way of him getting his comeuppance. She also had the integrity to never lead him in the wrong direction by allowing him to think that his logic wasn't flawed. She, like my Ole Dad, always gave him, us, something to think about... Yes there were times we got an ass whuppin' and there were many more times that it was explained, suggested or jokingly expressed to us how our choices could/would result in life whuppin' our ass. The older I become the more I respect my parents ability to help prepare me (and my siblings) for the life I'm leading today!

Teaching and training are two entirely different things. Teaching is like direct current in electricity; it goes one way from teacher to student. Training is like alternating current; it goes both directions as transferring, receiving and vice versa. Teaching involves information being disseminated while training involves hands on activities, being engaged, participation and interaction with that information. While all training involves teaching, not all teaching includes training. The emphasis on the Lieutenant's role within the 13/1-14 is to convey the importance that the learning the process involves not simply knowing certain information b.u.t. learning how to use it. From a parenting perspective, this is equivalent to letting our children know about certain information about Life and showing them how to live. One of the mantras my parents lived by was, "If you're wrong you're wrong. I'm not going to support you in wrongdoing just because you're my child." What this translated into is that I couldn't depend upon my parents to have my back and speak up for me if I was in the wrong, especially when it was something I (and they) already knew was wrong because we already discussed it. If what I did wrong wasn't previously discussed, they'd treat the results as a Lesson learned (willfully) and they'd always add-on some addendums just in case I still wasn't convinced. See, in my household we actually had 'family meetings' where my parents and 6 siblings would get together and just talk about various things. One of our favorite games my Ole Earth introduced to us was called 'The Book of Questions'. The Book of Questions was just that, a book of almost 300 questions about life situations where you had to give your perspective on what you would do in certain circumstances. For example, there might be a questions in there like, "If you had to lose one sense what would it be and why?" or "If you had 24 hours to live what 3 things would you do?" Boy that was fun and I didn't realize until I was probably in my twenties that my Ole Earth, the trained psychologist and sociologist, was using that 'game' as a way to profile us and assess our principles and values. It also provided many teachable moments for my parents to address some of these ideas that would be a problem for us now and somewhere down the line. My upbringing wasn't restricted or religious. I was raised to be aware, discerning and to take responsibility for the results of my choices.

Another valuable parenting methods my parents taught me was the ability to maintain their Integrity without co-signing BS; their ability to communicate, verbally or non-verbally, their stance on certain issues without alienating themselves from me as their child. We had our conflicts yet they did an excellent job at maintaining our relationship. For example, in high school I came home one time itchin' like I had fleas and my Ole Earth stopped me in the kitchen and asked me what's wrong. I said, "Nothing" and she looked me in the eye and said, "You better be happy you ain't get something you can't get rid of; you could've got the monster! Now I already told you about messin' with those 'skanks' out in the street. When you go upstairs you better not use any of our soap, rags, towels or toilet. You better ask one of your homeboys do they got something for that or go to the drugstore and get something to get rid of it." After that incident she'd joke with me once in a while about my lack of observation skills. She, nor my Ole Dad, never put themselves on a pedestal as if they never made poor choices and still didn't make poor choices. Most times they were very understanding and made it clear they were here to help guide us as their children -and they made many sacrifices to do so. They didn't just dictate what we should/shouldn't do nor did they sit back and let us say/do whatever we wanted; they had a wise way of giving us options to do things that they could live with. And if we took it too far, they'd always leave a lifeline if we wanted to come back. Rarely did they try to 'save us' from ourselves, especially when they already made knowledge born to us about what we got ourselves into. Some of the coddling, doting and co-signing I cee parents doing today with children who are oftentimes saying/doing things that are completely unacceptable or outright disrespectful was 'publically' rare when I was growing up. It was clear who the parent and who the child was. It was also clear who the parent was and who was no longer a child as they got older.

In my travels I've ceen and heard many parents defend certain principles and values to the death yet when their own child(ren) are doing the complete opposite they change their tune... They didn't change it because their child(ren) somehow gave them more insight into a phenomena they previously didn't understand. They changed their tune to make an exception or excuses because it's their child(ren). Basically it's not really that wrong or bad when "their child" is doing it so there was a biasness with "their child" that wasn't extended to other children. I've ceen parents talk about how wrong parents are for letting their teenage daughter get pregnant yet they're letting their teenage son's girlfriend spend the night over the house. I've heard parents throw boys under the bus about calling females "bitches", hear their own child saying "bitch" and they act like they don't even hear it. Maybe these parents don't know how to address these contradictions, maybe they're making exceptions/excuses because it's their child. Maybe they honestly don't cee the contradiction or maybe they really just don't even care. Whatever the reasoning is, if we're parents that advocate certain principles and values yet turn around and allow our child(ren) to undermine those principles and values within our household, we are signaling to them that these principles and values aren't worthy of being honored and respected in the first place. On a very practical level, this is the wrong attitude and information we're teaching our children and training them to take into the world. One of the main lessons our children should learn from us is 'integrity'. It is those children who don't learn this sense of fortitude (integrity) who become most receptive to the uninhibited ways of this world. There was never a time when my parents ignored something or turned a blind eye to something that was wrong. If they ceen or heard it they checked it and if it wasn't right & exact they weren't co-signing it or promoting it. This is not to say my parents were always right. There were definitely times me and my siblings had to educate them too and they weren't always receptive either. Because they always encouraged communication, they kept a good pulse on what was going on inside our hearts and heads. We couldn't just walk in or around the house not saying anything or keeping our thoughts and feelings to ourselves. Even if I wanted to my parents set up specific procedures, traditions and customs to keep our lives open and transparent. One of them was sitting down eating dinner together.

The bottom line is that the ultimate support we can give our children is the truth. If something isn't right & exact then let it be known and don't support what isn't. Sometimes our children already know what's up b.u.t. will present situations to us just to cee if we'll confirm what's right & exact. People do this all the time and they're somebody's child, so YES our children do it too! It's better for their feelings to be hurt about what's right then to let them walk around feeling good about what's wrong. Ignorance on our part or theirs must never be an option. As a parent, if something happened to them under those circumstances it would be hard to forgive yourself when you knew better (Ezekiel 3:18, St. Luke 12:47). Some parents interpret this to mean, "lock your child down" which is not what I'm saying, especially when they've reached their teens and are starting to assert their autonomy and make decisions on their own. At this stage in the game telling them what to do and how to do it is not the most effective way to deal with them. Don't believe me, try it and cee the results you'll get. At this stage it's more about our ability to negotiate, reason and walk them through the logic/illogic of their decisions. This is why I emphasized the importance of 'integrity'; it's difficult to negotiate, reason and walk someone through the logic/illogic of things that we haven't demonstrated a clear stance on. For example, it's difficult to check a teenager about running the streets if you're beating them out of the door and it's a challenge to teach your son about treating a woman like a Queen when you really aren't sure what a Queen is and don't talk about or treat men like Kings. These questions will come up and as parents we must be prepared and know how to handle these conversations. Telling a five year old, "Because I said so" may work b.u.t. for a teenager you probably just gave them a license to ill. Many of the dysfunctional relationships I cee between parents and children is simply because the children view us (parents) as consistent. Sometimes they have a legitimate reason why they think this because some of us actually are. Other times we've earned ourselves that title by default simply because we refused to check our children about some inconsistent behavior.

In conclusion, if we let things slide with our children we will slip as parents. My Ole Earth had a very humorous way of checking me that made me think about my decisions I've made or she suspected I might make WITHOUT telling what to do. She trusted my ability to discern because she and my Ole Dad invested time to equip me with the proper information to correct errors. When I went away to college they drove me 8 ½ hours away from home and dropped me off. It was for football camp, a month before classes started; the first time I saw this place and the first time I was that far away from home. I never felt so alone and was insecure about what to do but my parents obviously weren't. They had all the confidence in the world in me to make the best decisions with my Life and strive to do what's right & exact. Of course I didn't make those decisions all the time yet I made them enough to be here doing what I'm positively doing today. Even though some of you may have had a different upbringing or weren't able to depend upon your parents, you can change that with your children. Regardless how we were raised and where we came from it's important to be better for the next generation. This starts with being impartial to the truth. If you think homosexuality isn't right & exact then find an effective way to communicate this to your child that's doing it. It's wrong to criticize others for doing it and then get quiet or defensive when your own child's name comes up. Our children aren't always going to do what we expect them to do, we didn't do everything our parents expected us to do. There comes a point in our children's growth/development where the only resources they'll have from us to help them navigate and make sense of their lives is 1.) Our experiences and 2.) Our words echoing in the back of their mind. As parents, it's important to make sure these experiences are something we're willing to let them live with, and our Words are something we're willing to let them die for...

Tim Wise; Anti-Racist Activist and Writer

Caucasian Five Percenters

"Not only should they learn that our Nation (The NGE) is "Not Pro-Black or Anti-White" b.u.t. as a Caucasian, they first need to learn "I am Not Pro-White or Anti-Black"."

On June 26th, 2010 I wrote an article entitled 'Knowledge of Self Series' that contained a section elaborating on Five Percenters not being "Pro-Black or Anti-White". What I didn't elaborate on is the specific role that Caucasians play within our nation who do embrace our cultural worldview.

One of things that inspired me to write this article is because of the mainstream appeal our nation has gained over the years via community organizing, Hip Hop and online exposure. 40 plus years ago people generally had no idea who the Five Percenters (The NGE) were outside of the 5 Boroughs in NYC. Nowadays people in the Netherlands, Australia, China, Poland, South Africa, Pakistan, Texas, Mississippi, Pennsylvania, Chicago and many other places around the world contact me and various other Five Percenters I know about learning our way of life. Although many of these people are black/brown, there are also many Caucasians who reach out as well. So instead of addressing these segments of the population individually I wanted to provide this information to answer some of their Frequently Asked Questions (FAQ). Another thing that inspired me is the fact that there are some Caucasians who know or are studying our cultural curriculum and I wanted to give them more insight into their specific role as civilized people. I also wanted to clarify this to other Five Percenters who may be unclear about the specific role of Caucasian Five Percenters in our nation.

120 Lessons, the core of our cultural curriculum, consists of people, places and things that inform original (black/brown) people about our primary identity, role and place in the Universe and on the map of human geography. When a

Caucasian is introduced to this cultural curriculum they discover from the very beginning that they are not primary (original) and have a different identity, a different role and inhabit different places upon this map of human geography. Since 'God' and the 'Earth; existed long before non-melanated (Caucasians) people were born, the fundamental question that arises is, "Since they can't be God or the Earth, what status do Caucasians have and purpose do they serve within the context of our nation?"

The Caucasus Mountains

Knowledge of Self (KOS)

I know many Five Percenters whose ancestors come from different places throughout the planet earth. Some come from India, China, Puerto Rico, Jamaica, Trinidad, Ghana, Mexico, Ethiopia, 6 Nations (or other indigenous lands) and various places throughout North America like Detroit, Los Angeles, Dallas, Windsor, Florida, Indianapolis, Chicago, Alabama, Seattle, Toronto and etc... Because they come from different places and have different experiences, they all bring a unique perspective, lineage and story about our original people from these places throughout the earth. If I want more insight into the chronology of our original people in the Dominican Republic all I need to do is reach out to a Five Percenter whose direct ancestry comes from this location; they can tell me any and everything I need to know. If I need to do more research on any of these countries, states or cities, I look no further than my brothers/sisters as primary contacts who are native to that geographic location; they usually know or have direct access to the language, idioms, customs, climate, social norms, demographics and anything else about this place their family is originally from. In otherwords, this is 'Knowledge of Self' (KOS) that puts our cultural curriculum in the proper context. When I was out in Seattle doing a Speaking Engagement/Book Signing with Sujan Dass (Supreme Understanding), he spoke on the importance of having this sense of Knowledge of Self and how we each approach this cultural curriculum from the vantage point of the ethnic identity, socioeconomics and geographic location we and our family came from.

This idea of KOS is not new and has always been the Standard and a national consensus amongst us since the earliest years of the nation. When the Father and his companions began teaching in NYC there were so-called Latin American brothers/sisters who naturally identified with this cultural worldview and often faced criticism/rejection by those of us who didn't cee our Spanish speaking original people as black also. Many of these criticisms/rejections were put to rest when these Spanish speaking original people began to educate themselves and those critics about the chronology of our people in places like Puerto Rico, Cuba and etc... Thus we all began to better understand another unique perspective, lineage and story of our (original) people that was already identified within our lessons. As this culture spread beyond the 5 Boroughs, other original people from different places began to add on and also include their unique chapter in the chronology of our nation. While Caucasians are also identified within our lessons, the same standard and national consensus is expected of those of them who unnaturally identify with our cultural worldview and desire to gain KOS. So the questions they must ask/answer for themselves are, "What unique perspective, lineage and story do

I (a Caucasian) have in relationship to original people?" and "What am I doing as a Caucasian to put the criticisms/rejections to rest that the majority of the people on the planet earth and the earth itself have about my group of people?"

Azrael, a Caucasian whom the Father taught, established the first prototypical model of how Caucasians were educated and allowed to minimally function within the context of our national body. Azrael will tell you in a minute that the name he was given means "Death Angel" (Angel of Death), he symbolically holds the keys to heaven and hell and his job is to help show us (original people and other Caucasians) how to survive the traps of this devilish world his people were allowed to make. He also understands the position/status he was given to primarily educate his own people to the truth about who they are, who we are and what his people need to do in order to help establish/secure a world of peace where they can co-exist with us as one human family. I can respect that and have personally referred Caucasians to him. Unlike Azrael, I've noticed that "95%" (14, 15/1-40) of the other Caucasians I cee who're interested in studying or who do study our cultural curriculum are usually unclear about what they're supposed to be doing. Many of them haven't even realized or been taught that they're supposed to be sharing their unique perspective, lineage and story as a Caucasian and how this ultimately defines/impacts their role/purpose within our nation. Instead of acknowledging and elaborating on their actual historical identity, role and place within 120 lessons like a God/Earth with Native American, Indian, Iranian or etc. ancestry does, they'll identify themselves generically and non-politically. In other words, they'll talk about everything b.u.t. their actual identity, role and place within our lessons. Instead they'll share abstract scientific theories and philosophize about who/what things symbolically mean. If they do "put a face on" something they'll usually engage in conversations with us (original people) trying to tell us about ourselves and how we cee things. An example of this is if they're asked about "Who wrote the holy koran or bible? How long ago and why does Islam renew its history every 25,000 years?" they'll attempt to tell us about ourselves; the black man and woman of Asia, not what this means to them, their woman, people and how they're consequently on our time. Although it's important for them to know who/what we are, it's most important for them to recognize who they are and have historically been to us and their own people. That is their primary point of view. I've rarely heard them directly talking about how they cee "our" lessons in relationship to themselves, their people, their history and their relationship to my people. I rarely hear these Caucasians explaining their identity as a grafted man, why Musa had such a hard time civilizing them, how it effects them to be genetically weak boned/weak blooded, at what points in history their people's identity/behavior codifies devilishment and what are some of the psychological, social and cultural challenges that come along with the inability to be God or the Earth. I'm sure thoughts/feelings like these and many others arise in Caucasians because there is no other way to view our lessons than from their own perspective and experience. So for a Caucasian to not engage/participate in these important discussions by sharing their perspective and experiences it says:

1.) They're not being properly educated.
2.) They're not really striving to be educated and want to come amongst us for other reasons.

Regardless what the reason is, whenever someone isn't actively engaged, participating or involved they're not receiving the necessary training to effectively perform their duty. In our case, we call that duty "civilization" and our stance "righteousness". It also must be understood that historically speaking, a Caucasian's inability to effectively perform a duty as noble as civilization and righteousness has always translated into the worse fate for any original people, their own people and the environment that's in proximity to them. Among various other lessons we learn, our 1st, 4th, 9th and 10th degrees in 1/1-14 and 34th & 38th degrees in the 1-40 provide structural models and plans of recourse to specifically address issues like this.

Because of the unsavory relationship Caucasians have historically had towards original people, other Caucasians and the planet earth itself, their journey towards becoming civilized and righteous requires reaching and training units specific to them. In order to be civilized and righteous, there are many things, tangible (objects/possessions) and intangible (ideas/allegiances), they must relinquish and denounce that does not coincide with civilization and righteousness; white priviledge. Since, according to our 8th degree in the 1-14, they (Caucasians) kept/keep our people (original people) apart from their own social equality. There are many institutional, educational, psychological, socioeconomic, labor, legal and military opportunities Caucasians must be committed to sharing with us wheh they coincide with our culture. If Caucasians think being a Five Percenter means to come around us, learn how we talk and then talk it back to us so they can be accepted they have it wrong! They're not honorary Gods and Earths. They are exactly who our lessons and chronology says they are and they came to us to "learn to do like the original man (and woman)" because they want to clean up their people's global image. If we (original people) think that teaching Caucasians means training them to parrot our lessons and simply explain who we are as God and the Earth we have it wrong too! Some of us may sit back and feel accomplished to be able to say, "Here's a Caucasian who acknowledges that the black man is God and the black woman is the Earth" yet it says nothing about who they are, what their thoughts/feelings are in regard to their own identity/history and what type of behavior this actually translates into. Our lessons (17, 18/1-36) clearly teach us that in the early 1930's there were approximately 3 million Caucasians who also acknowledged who we were yet their thoughts/feelings about who they were in relationship to us still translated into uncivilized and unrighteous behavior; segregation (8/1-14) was going on, Jim Crow etiquette was expected, the Klu Klux Klan (KKK) had over 2.5 Million card carrying members and anti-lynching legislation was debated/unenforced. We also must consider the fact that many agent provocateurs (4/1-14) were able to successfully infiltrate, undermine and sabotage the objectives/goals of our organizations and colonize our lands because we simply allowed them to come amongst us without a thorough investigation and requiring them to announce themselves through sharing their perspective, lineage and story. This is not to say nor assume that this is every Caucasian's or even an original person's intention. This is to say that anytime we've taken this ass-umptive posture, especially with those who are clearly unalike, it's always been a recipe for disaster.

In closing, "We are Not Pro-Black or Anti-White" is not a statement that means we're a bunch of Humanists saying "Can we all just get along?" This declaration does not mean we're trying to assimilate into the dominant society/culture, we don't want to offend white people and we're striving to distance ourselves from so-called 'black militants'. This statement means that our allegiance is to the truth, wherever it may exist, and we're required to do what's most civilized and righteous in accordance to the truth "regardless to whom or what" (11/1-14). This is my position and posture as an original man and this stance requires me to interface with a western society that historically opposed and still opposes this view. A Caucasian is someone who represents this western society; genotypically and phenotypically. Therefore, their allegiance to the truth, wherever it may exist, and what they're required to do that's most civilized and righteous takes on a different meaning. Not only should they learn that our nation is "Not Pro-Black or Anti-White" b.u.t. as a Caucasian, they first need to learn "I am Not Pro-White or Anti-Black". Just because a Caucasian can recite or even write RZA like lyrics like his verse on the Gravediggaz "The Night The Earth Cried" it doesn't mean they're not Pro-White; they could be still be gettin' money working for their family business that has historically discriminated against original people. Just because a Caucasian man has a black girlfriend or bi-racial child doesn't mean he's not Anti-Black; he could be f*cking her and still saying f*ck her family and original people as a whole. The beauty in our cultural worldview is that our Lessons clearly exposes someone's position and posture be it 'Pro' or 'Anti' anything that doesn't coincide with the truth. When it comes to Caucasians, if they're not learning to analyze and articulate their historical identity, role and place as a Caucasian in this world, then what purpose can they possibly serve to us? If some of you have/are teaching them our lessons, mathematics, alphabets and etc. yet they aren't consistently demonstrating in their daily people activities (amongst their own people) or actively taking stances to show & prove that they are not Pro-White or Anti-Black then they're not performing the duty of a civilized/righteous person; they're upholding the uncivilized/unrighteous status quo of their Ancestors. Are they here to just sit around the fathers and mothers of civilization and agree with us about who we say we are? Are we nothing more than a cultural confession box so Caucasians can come around and confess their and their ancestors sins against God and the Earth? Like Azrael, do they have a specific job amongst their own people and what does their job specifically entail? I remember I went to a rally in Bethlehem (Buffalo, NY) one time and this Caucasian female who called herself an 'Earth' came out and wanted to learn more about our culture. Apparently some original man was teaching her who got some lessons from a God who hadn't ceen him in years. When I asked her about her ancestry she said she was 'Irish' and I began asking her some questions about her people's history and their history in relationship to original people. She couldn't tell me anything about this or her status as a Caucasian in western society yet she knew some of the Supreme Mathematics, things about our nation and how to use some of our phrases... I shared alittle history about Ireland, the Irish and Caucasians as a group and then informed her to do more research on her people so she can begin to better understand how she's been taught to cee the world and consequently the fathers and mothers of civilization. That was the last time I ceen/heard anything from her. She's probably still out there along with many other Caucasians and original people who continue to be uneducated and miseducated about 'What We Teach' and 'What We Will Achieve' as a Nation of Gods and Earths. The only way to change this reality is for us to continue our tradition of requiring people to show & prove who and what they are, not just in word b.u.t. in deed through what they "continue daily" to do. (13/1-40)

Studiousness; To Study

"Study to shew thyself approved" -2nd Timothy Chapter 2 Verse 15

What happened to studiousness? More often than not, I come across people in person and read some of the things they're posting and/or commenting about online and that's the first thought that goes through my mind, "What happened to studiousness?" When I was getting KOS (Knowledge of Self) during the pre-Google days, I'd spend hours in the library doing research on the lessons I was learning. I was never handed a bunch of paper, told to memorize this information and then sent on my merry little way. Studiousness was the order of the day. On many occasions I'd build with my enlightener until the Sun was coming up the next day and sometimes he'd wake me up in the middle of the night to build or quote a lesson. I couldn't stand it at the time, b.u.t. I learned to appreciate that later on in life - especially in an era like today. So when I hear Ghost's verse on 'Rainy Dayz' where he says, "*Stood up late nights/build with my A-Alikes*" I lived that out, taught and teach this way. Many Five Percenters whom I know, that are usually the most studious, can relate to staying up late nights as well. That type of investment is a sacred bond and that level of commitment to another person's life deserves the upmost honor & respect. This brotherly/sisterly love is the cornerstone our nation was built upon and keystone of our God centred cultural worldview. As reflected in the sequence of our 10th, 11th and 12th Jewels; when we're unable to give/receive this type of love in a relationship, we'll never attain real peace and true happiness in our lives.

I was recently involved in a discussion online about the importance of considering 'policy' & 'procedure' when effectively addressing national concerns and someone dismissed my point by saying, "Our nation isn't run like a government." The first thought that came to my mind is that they're overlooking the 18th letter in the Supreme Alphabet 'Rule or Ruler'; words that mean 'to govern' and the role of 'a governor.' This is the prefix to the word 'government'. It's impossible to 'Rule' or even be a 'Ruler' over our own habits, desires, urges and challenges if we don't have the ability to 'govern' these habits, desires, urges and challenges. Since this was overlooked then I'm also sure they didn't make this correlation: Without a system of government it's impossible to effectively perform/reinforce the "duty of a civilized person" (18/1-40) because there's no formal structure governing civil 'policy' & 'procedure.' In other words, any group of people without a civil service (government) become anarchistic (lawless/savage).

It was this incident and various others that further convinced me that many of my people, for whatever reason, aren't being studious enough. And not only are we not being studious b.u.t. many of us don't realize that this is the order of the day. Not because "I" (Saladin) say it's the order of the day b.u.t. because what we call ourselves (God/Earth, King/Queen, civilized, righteous, just & true, allwise, right & exact and etc.) demands this level of consideration. Another thing to consider is that primitive people had to learn (evolve) a system of organized government and civil codes in order to become a nation -as highlighted in the 2, 4, 5, 9/1-14. Their level of adherence to a system of civil codes defines/marks their level of civilization. According to the 2, 4/1-14 specifically, without this knowledge an environment becomes a geographic landscape for "savages living a beast way of life" because there are no identifiable Rules (governing mechanisms). Did not Musa come to teach them "how to 'live respectful lives' and how to 'build homes' for themselves"? Well these are 'Rules' in the form of social norms/mores and a 'Ruler' in regards to a tool used to properly measure/build a shelter. So to even state that our nation is not run like a government reveals that many of us are still entertaining very primitive ideas about nation building. The only problem with this lack of maturity/growth is when these people are content with this lot in life and aren't striving to evolve.

Because Information appears to be so readily accessible online today, many of the Five Percenters who have gotten and are getting KOS in the Google era aren't doing the work by going to their local libraries, investing in resources or developing relationships anymore. Many of these people are becoming more anti-social, alienated and disassociated from other human beings; which is the complete antithesis to learning our way of life (culture) and improving the conditions of our families/communities. The sacredness of establishing a lifelong relationship of brother/sisterhood has now turned into people thinking it's all about you just handing them some information, downloading documents online or talking on the phone. Learning to communicate a system of principles and values we live and die by has now turned into people wanting to learn how to talk/sound like us. From my short experience of being in this nation amongst my contemporaries, I can boldly say that many of our cultural traditions/customs are becoming loss. Their lack of transmittance to our present and future generations also threatens what we've achieved and are striving to achieve as a nation. Many of us today don't even realize that we actually have a collective purpose or goals we're striving to achieve. Many people think that 'getting Knowledge of Self' means 'getting Knowledge for myself personally' -even though someone made sacrifices and invested valuable time to share it with them...

So whose fault is this? Is it the enlightener's fault for not being studious/committed enough to demand a level of studiousness/commitment in the people they're so-called teaching? Possibly. Is it the so-called student's fault for not having the proper attitude about relationships and demonstrating the aptitude to actually learn? Yeah that's possible too. Is it our elders fault for not stepping up to the plate and staying relevant by reinforcing our traditions/customs instead of being retired builders? No doubt. Is it Five Percenters fault collectively for not moving towards a more organized structure (governing body)? Absolutely. There is enough blame to go around for everybody b.u.t. ultimately WE ARE ALL RESPONSIBLE. We are responsible for what we claim to be (Gods/Earths) and we're responsible to those who desire to represent these standards and cultural worldview. If not, then who? If us, then when?

In closing I want to encourage those of us who consider ourselves Five Percenters, those who're in the process of learning our culture and those who want to learn our culture to understand that studiousness is the order of the day. Many of our cultural perspectives are not being transmitted simply because many people are not studying. I'm not talking about knowing the Father's born day, who taught who in Medina or why our Universal Flag has 22 points. Although history is important, it should not be used like it's a game of Jeopardy. It's likewise important to study the lessons we were all taught to memorize/recite by heart. These lessons comprise 80% of our cultural worldview; the mass from which we derive our perspectives about life from. Our Supreme Mathematics and Supreme Alphabet are numerical and alphabetical systems used to help us compute, calculate, give cultural context to and communicate these perspectives. We can't claim "knowledge is our foundation" and not study -especially basic words (concepts) in our Supreme Alphabet like 'Rule or Ruler' and then expect to effectively perform/reinforce civil duties (18/1-40) that support our nation. We can't claim titles like King/Queen and not research the appropriate principles (policies), approaches (procedures) and attitudes (etiquette) that support

our ability to uphold that title. To be 'studious' means we must remain 'students', always willing to learn (evolve) in order to serve an even greater purpose to our families, community, people and the world.

The Harlem Renaissance

A Community of Self

Efficacy is our ability to succeed in a particular situation or produce certain results. In considering self efficacy, the basic question one must ask is, *"What is the purpose for our personal accomplishments/achievements and our intention to produce certain results?"* In other words, the question of 'purpose/function' is of the upmost importance when discussing efficacy. Why? Because what someone is actually doing or the purpose they're fulfilling IS their efficacy (their capacity to produce) -or lack thereof. Therefore, we can't truly talk/intellectualize about self efficacy, we have to be about it, and being about it means our lifestyle demonstrates our efficacy via actual contributions we've made and consistently make to civilization. If you're interested in learning about fitness then consult with an actual fitness instructor or a person who actually includes physical fitness as an integral part of their lifestyle. If you do consult with someone who's obviously not about fitness, you'll probably get a whole bunch of unrelated opinions and criticisms about physical fitness & character assassination of those people who are physically fit. They'll also give you a slew of excuses why fitness is subjective and relatively unimportant as a method to justify and divert attention away from their own apathy, lack of discipline, inactivity and unhealthy behaviors. Sometimes people like this even go as far as to pride themselves on how sick/unhealthy they are by proclaiming how much they love doing what they do -regardless how it's negatively effecting them, their companions, their families, their community or society as a whole.

So any true exploration of efficacy is an examination of relationships; how a person relates to Self, others and the environment. This is one very important key that is highlighted/implied in the story of Yacub. His family relationships were dysfunctional: there was no mention of his parents/guardians or potential siblings and he was born 20 miles outside of civilization or where knowledge (1) and wisdom (2) or 'love' started. His social relationships were unstable: there was no mention of any friends, siblings or associates and he played by himself. His academic relationships were questionable: he was considered a high achiever and praised Academia yet there was no mention or credence shown to any mentors/benefactors. His societal and community relationships were isolated: he was born outside of civilization and he lived on an island called Pelon (Patmos) for over 100 years away from civilization inoculated against any outside influences. These conditions/conditionings imply why this type of person would have a 'Big-Head' (egotism, grandiosity, narcissism and an inferiority complex). This is the same psychological profile of someone who is suffering from forms of Mental Illnesses such as anti-social behavior, napoleon complex, manic-depression, obsessive compulsive behavior, reactive attachment disorder and etc. These are the same Illnesses that sets the stage for not only manufacturing devils b.u.t. also crimes against humanity (serial murders, identity theft, rape, sexual deviancy, larceny and etc.) and the environment (pollution, animal cruelty, littering, increasing their carbon footprint and etc.). Is there any wonder why Yacub means 'to supplant or undermine' or why people like this promote subversive, obstructive, disruptive and destructive ideologies? If you take a moment and simply listen to a person's ideals, their complaints and how they're participating in this world, you may actually hear them speaking from the vantage point of Pelon (an island)... So although Yacub being successful in all "his" undertakings does constitute a level of efficacy, the question of 'purpose/function' is of the upmost importance; are the results he produced conducive to sustaining and progressing our relationship with Self, others and the environment? (29/1-40) Some may argue "Yes" by saying, "The 38/1-40 teaches us that Yacub's 'purpose/function' ultimately allows us to "show forth and prove our power that we are all wise and righteous... without falling victim" and I have to agree with that. The people arguing this point must also agree with me that in order to make that claim we must be demonstrating this power, wisdom and righteousness to not fall victim... If we're not striving to demonstrate this, then we're only lip professin' followers of Yacub. What I'm sharing represents some of those "other rules and regulations" of Yacub's that are not mentioned in that lesson. (28/1-40)

I'm always contacted by people from all over the world who're interested, curious about and intrigued by Supreme Mathematics, Supreme Alphabets, 120 lessons or my culture as a whole. When asked what their reasoning is for learning I've heard everything from, *"Knowledge is like money and I'm just trying to get that money"*, *"I want to enhance my music career"*, *"I want to get more confidence"*, *"Because I think you're the most qualified"*, *"My boyfriend won't teach me"*, *"I don't know"*, *"I want to teach others"* and etc.. Whatever a person's reasoning is, there is one thing that is fundamental to them being educated; sharing. All of us who claim to have Knowledge of Self only have it because someone shared it; directly/indirectly. Even if we claim we did it on our own (19: Self or Savior), ANYTHING we have is a part of someone else's contributions. Whatever interpretation we claim to have, regardless how unique or personal we declare it to be, it is still 'intertexual'. When it comes to basic sharing, even the toiletries we have/use were made possible via the efforts of others and without their contributions we would have to figure out other ways to maintain our cleanliness/health. As individuals (truly meaning 'not divided'), we are only as "healthy, strong and good" as the group (people, family, community and society) we contribute to and receive resources from (28/1-40). If Life was essentially about "coming" by myself (2/1-36), human beings would be asexual... And if you took a cursory glance at the psychological and socioeconomic "hard times, hunger, nakedness and out of doors" people experience, you'll often cee a direct link to a living single mentality (11/1-40). I mention this to emphasize that in order to gain anything, we must have a healthy respect for the sacredness/sacrifices that comes along with receiving what others have shared. Some people receive what they consider Knowledge of Self and don't hold it sacred nor do they make sacrifices to share it like the ones whom they received it from. Some people want you to share with them yet don't have any intention of sharing their goals, experiences and basic lives with you. Sometimes people have the misconception that Knowledge of Self is some "thing" you hand them and once they get "it" from you they go on their way and do whatever they want with "it". The reality is, we are establishing lifelong relationships based upon growth & development principles and Values -with the determined idea of establishing these lifelong relationships with others. From our cultural perspective, we are helping eachother become viable/productive members of our society; not anti-socialists, hedonists, misers or rugged individuals. Our society, The NGE, is based upon a culture that establishes a system of community life where its persons form a collective, continual and regulating body to mutually benefit, progress and protect its interests. This sets the stage to associate; based upon the common cultural status, ideals, language, experiences and interests we share. If this wasn't the underlining significance of our culture, there would be no integrity and nothing would get transmitted (shared), established or protected from one person to the next... Again, efficacy especially self efficacy is not simply about someone's personal capacity to produce certain results, it's about the sustainability and progressiveness of the relationships we produce from those results.

In conclusion, keep in mind that we are all a part of a cycle of life and all things, whether animate or inanimate, are interdependent. As great as Michael Jordan was as a 'single' player, there is no Michael Jordan without a team, mentors, food, oxygen, textile companies or parents who gave birth to him. It's not about how smart we think we are, it's about what we're actually doing to use our smarts to help improve the intelligence of others. It's not about how good we think we are in something, it's about how we're using our ability to help others become better in what they do.

Frankenstein Mob

None Dare Call It Conspiracy?

"Congress shall make no law respecting an establishment of religion, or prohibiting the free exercise thereof; or abridging the freedom of speech, or of the press; or the right of the people peaceably to assemble, and to petition the government for a redress of grievances."

The above paragraph is the First Amendment of the US Constitution's Bill of Rights in regards to freedom of speech, press, religion and petition. Under this Amendment, it guarantees freedom of religion yet also requires the separation between the church and state. This has far reaching implications and is very important for people to understand, especially those who don't claim a "religion" but a cultural worldview and nationality. As for Five Percenters (AKA: the Nation of Gods and Earths), we are not a religion or a religious group. We are not Muslims and we advocate a God-centered "cultural" worldview. Even though the Federal District Court in New York ruled that Intelligent Tareef Allah had been denied his First Amendment Right of religious freedom, and is entitled to practice our culture in prison, this court decision represents an exception. In many correctional facilities across the United States, Five Percenters are labeled a 'gang' and 'STG' (Security Threat Group). This is the ruling perspective of the dominant class and what they consider to be their status quo. While this perspective is obviously unfair/unreasonable -in light of the many Five Percenters who are positive/progressive members in their families, communities and society as a whole-, some of these claims are not without merit. Like in many societies, there do exist segments (pockets) of people who claim to beFive Percenters who knowingly/unknowingly reinforce these stigmas -based upon their own immature, amoral, uncivilized and irresponsible behavior.

In the early developmental years of Allah's Five Percent, the youth were the 99% who responded to this cultural worldview. These youth were middle schoolers, high schoolers and dropouts. Most weren't fathers/mothers, college graduates, home owners or business owners. They were learning, often for the very first time, the responsibilities of manhood and womanhood. While going through this urban rights of passage, they were simultaneously being introduced to the apex of manhood/womanhood; Kings/Queens and Gods/Earths. While some of these youth excelled in this educational process, many of them didn't meet some of these challenges that came along with being immature/inexperienced (young) and dealing with the obvious socioeconomic turbulence of the 1960's. Magnify this with the claim of 'culture freedom', and this alienated many of these youth or put them in direct opposition to various religious, nationalistic and secular groups/organizations who viewed this stance as a direct threat to their doctrine, cultural identity and social status. The Father (FKA: Clarence 13X) was viewed not only as a pied piper of sorts, but also a potential enemy of the state and threat to the US government. Why? Because of his clearly non-religious cultural stance in the midst of a Christian country that advocates a Eurocentric cultural status quo. So legally speaking, the Father, his companions and the youth they mentored had no real protection under the First Amendment of the US Constitution's Bill of Rights in regards to freedom of speech, press, religion and petition. When you examine the stances that many other people took who veered away from a "religious" perspective into a cultural/nationalistic arena, you'll notice something very consistent. Garvey was deported (exiled) for so-called mail fraud, Noble Drew Ali was mysteriously murdered, when Martin Luther King Jr. started talking about the African Diaspora he got shot in Memphis, El Hajj Malik Shabazz (Malcom X.) was assassinated not long after he started the Organization of African Unity and began talking about taking the issue of black people's human rights to the United Nations, COINTELPRO dismantled the Black Panther Party, the Philadelphia Police Dept. dropped a bomb on the MOVE Organization destroying 65 homes killing 11 adults/children, a healthy Dr. Khalid Abdul Muhammad (spokesman of the New Black Panther Party) died from mysterious "natural causes" and the leader of the Nuwaubian nation is sitting in a Supermax Prison in Florence Colorado as you read this article. In regards to Five Percenters; within two short years of being arrested at a rally on false charges and his name added to the FBI Security Index, the Father was sent to Bellevue Hospital for psychiatric treatment, sentenced to Mattewan State Hospital for the criminally insane and assassinated not long after being released and effectively politicizing our national agenda and cultural worldview. Many Caucasians clearly got the memo because some years later

Scientologists, Satanists and Wiccans sought legal protection under the First Amendment by establishing "churches"; Church of Scientology, Church of Satan and various Wiccan Churches. You even had White Supremacist groups establishing churches to get this protection such as The Creativity Movement (formally known as The World Church of the Creator). So ask yourself the question, "Where does this still leave those who don't claim a 'religion' but a cultural worldview and nationality?"

On December 31, 2011, President Barack Obama signed into Law HR Bill 1540. While this massive 900 plus page document covers the ins and outs of national defense, the most controversial part of this bill is the counterterrorism section (Subtitle D). It allows arbitrary and indefinite detainment of those who're classified as domestic/foreign terrorist suspects, yes "suspects" as in, "we think you're saying/doing something." Bill 1540 also specifies that the US is engaged in armed conflict with not only Al-Qaeda and the Taliban b.u.t. other associated forces that pose a threat to the US, it's citizens and it's allied forces (coalition partners). Also, these "forces" the US are in conlfict with are defined as any 'belligerent' nations, organizations or persons engaged in 'hostilities' against the US, it's citizens and it's allied forces (coalition partners). The problem with such language is that it's very broad. Anyone that's posting 'belligerent' comments over Facebook, uploading what can be considered 'hostile' videos on Youtube, or even having loud tactless conversations around people about your nationalistic pride can possibly earn them free transportation to an island prison, denied your civil rights and eventually brought before a military court to answer for your suspected sins (10/1-14). While President Obama offered his obvious reservations while signing this bill into law, this says nothing about the sentiments/reasoning of his administration, congress, the military or the next administration that gets into office after his terms are over. This also says nothing about the state/local government's sentiments/reasoning in the cities where we live. What this all translates into is this: Anyone who doesn't claim a "religion" but a cultural worldview and nationality must be wiser in how/what you are openly advocating. I think many of us black/brown people forget that we are historical prisoners of war. Black people in particular, many who didn't migrate to this country but whose ancestors were brought here as slaves, must be aware of this. In the 239 years the United States has existed, black people were legally denied basic human and civil rights to participate in this society for 189 of those years. It wasn't until 1965, a little over a generation ago (50 short years) that legislation was passed to end legal segregation, on paper at least yet not in principle nor in perspective. In other words, we were and still are behind socioeconomic, religious, and cultural enemy lines and anything we say/do has been and can be used against us in "their" court of law. From some of the events that have occured in my life as a public figure, I'm sure there's a dossier in my name and I'm also sure there's dossiers in other people's names who are far less considerate of what they're publically or privately saying/doing -whether they're calling their antics entertainment or not. Also, with an investigation into a possible 'hate crime' commmited against a God named 'Supreme' (Aakir Omar Ali) on January 3rd, it's important to be aware of our environment and how we may be open targets. Supreme was found face down burning alive off of Highway 64 in James City County Virginia and the only way of identifying him was via his dental records. The police department has released photos of his tattoos to generate possible leads/motives in this case, and one of his tattoos was of our Universal Flag.

In closing, I urge all of you to be more mindful of the political shifts in this society and what this may mean to you, your family and your community. Check out political blogs, news coverage and even strive to attend your local council meetings. Little by little, become more knowledgeable of your local, state, regional and national politics. This is especially important to those who can be considered "20 miles outside", living on the cultural fringes of this society (21/1-40). Since 9/11, America has become more patriotic than it's ever been and anything that remotely sounds like you don't like baseball or apple pie can have people advocating for one common cause to chase you out of town like Mary Shelley's Frankenstein. Some of us confuse national pride with cultural menticide. Yelling to the top of our lungs about who we claim to be while unassuming people stand around trying to figure out what size target to put on our back is not a question of pride. If you are a so-called revolutionary, that military strategy is equivalent to standing unarmed in an open field screaming for the enemy to come and get you. As I've stated, black/brown people have been behind enemy lines since we've been in this country. The historical 'belligerence' and 'hostility' we've received as a people shows & proves this to be the rule, not the exception. This has been the racial paradigm and power dynamics between the ruling class and underclass within this society since its inception (3, 4/1-10). Therefore much of the legislation, policies being and procedures being implemented does not consider the underclass. A company called Hibernia Atlantic has decided to build a $300 million dollar transatlantic fiber optic cable that will give companies a 60 millisecond 'inside trader' advantage of information being transferred overseas. Why mention this? Because project express will accelerate Wallstreet (and the global market), impact/modify the strategies of the Occupy Movement, and alter the sociopolitical landscape on the state/federal levels. At the beginning of 2012 many states, mostly southern, legalized mandatory voter photo ID laws. Although it's been reasoned that this will ensure less of a chance for voter fraud, which wasn't significant enough to even propose this type of law in the first place, this legislation will obviously suppress the voting capabilities of those people who either don't have a photo ID or find it very difficult to secure one; the elderly, minorities and youth. All you need to do is check the racial/age demographics in the states that were most adamant about getting this law passed. The bottom line is when we are unaware of these societal shifts, us, our family and our communities become vulnerable to the legal consequences of this ignorance. This is not a call to assimilate, hide, live in fear or be spooked out. This is a call for us to be more aware of our status, the politics and the socioeconomic climate of the society we live in. We will be better prepared to address legislation, policies and procedures being implemented that does not consider us or potentially target us. Ignorance isn't bliss, ignorance is a risk to our life, the lives of our family members and the livelihood of our community.